M000295397

DUDES OF WAR

DUDES OF WAR

⋮

BENJAMIN TUPPER

Epigraph Books
Rhinebeck, New York

Dudes of War © 2010 by Ben Tupper
All rights reserved. No part of this book may be used or reproduced in
any manner without written permission from the author except in critical
articles and reviews. Contact the publisher for information.

Printed in the United States of America

Cover photograph by Rafal Gerszak
Book and cover design by Georgia Dent

Library of Congress Control Number: 2010940186

ISBN: 978-0-9830517-3-2

Epigraph Books
27 Lamoree Road
Rhinebeck, New York 12572
www.epigraphPS.com
USA 845-876-4861

Dedicated to our fallen brother Master Sergeant Bernard "Deg" Deghand, whose soldierly ways were an inspiration to everyone who served with him.

Killed in Action, Spera, Afghanistan, September 15, 2006

Captain Cain and Corporal Polanski hang a plaque in memory of MSG Bernard Deghand, FOB Ghazni, Afghanistan

CONTENTS

INTRO TO A WAR STORY
THAT DOESN'T GO *BANG*

Welcome to a war story where nothing goes *bang*. That's not to say you're in for the memoirs of a fobbit who sat behind a desk for a year in Afghanistan and fought paper cuts and computer viruses. But consider it a fair warning for readers looking for tales of blood and guts. If reading about combat is your kick, then you are way off target with *Dudes of War*. Grab your receipt and return to wherever you purchased this book and pick up something else instead. I told all my combat stories in my offering *Greetings From Afghanistan, Send More Ammo*. This second book shoots an entirely different azimuth: To tell the story of the other 99 percent of the time we spend over there; the tasks, chores, and austere conditions that forge today's modern soldier culture.

It's this huge majority of non-combat time where we develop our unique rituals, habits, and hobbies that make a soldier a soldier. Living practically on top of each other in cramped, dirty quarters known as hootches, deprived of the creature comforts of home, we improvise, adapt, and overcome in ways that should amaze (and shock) civilians back home. The result is a Petri dish of soldier-isms: Things that feed our basic needs for all the things we are missing (mainly women, beer, and other forms of entertainment). Many of our improvisations, as you will read, are things that back home Mom would frown on. But while we are here, we do what we need to do to cut the stress of war and spice up the monotony of our daily life on the forward operating base (FOB).

So that's the focus: Life back in the hootch, the downtime, the pranks, the vices, and the events that cause the rib-cracking laughs that make war manageable. *Dudes of War* is an unashamed and personal look into our lives at war and it comes with some risks. First and foremost is the blowback from a handful of my veteran comrades who I write about who feel that what happened in Afghanistan stays in Afghanistan. A few of them, after having read some of these stories, made it clear they felt sharing these experiences with a civilian audience was a mistake. One felt embarrassed that his quirks were being put up for public analysis and review, even though I have presented him and all my subjects only by nickname, thus assuring their anonymity.

Another complained that these stories, as well intentioned as they may be, "do not transfer over to civilian life or experiences...because people weren't there...and they don't get it. " He clearly fears a backlash by the civilian population toward the military service member if some of our more controversial habits come to light. He cautioned me about my goal in educating the civilian side. He had long given up trying to educate the "other" (his word for civilians). While I don't doubt his frustrated past attempts to educate the other, the conclusion I have drawn is the opposite of his. Civilian society doesn't shun the soldier. To the contrary, civilian society thirsts for critical war memoirs, war movies, and military-themed video games. Civilians long to better understand the complexities of military life and soldier culture at war.

The problem of civilians not understanding military culture is a result of not enough combat veterans telling their stories in an open, uncensored, and unashamed voice. Too many times we let Hollywood or fiction writers fill in the truth gap. Hopefully, *Dudes of War* can serve to also fill this gap, except this time with firsthand accounts of soldier life and culture written by a guy who has been there, done that, and got the T-shirt.

In the end, an honest and revealing personal account of soldiers at war is a highly volatile subject to write about, and it generates stories that are simultaneously heroic, callous, cruel, and confused. To my comrades in arms who disagree with my candid sharing of these experiences here, or challenge the objectivity of my interpretations of the lessons learned from them—well, they have every right to pen their own war stories with their own perspectives, biases, and conclusions.

In closing, this exploration of life on our dusty, dirty and ramshackle forward operating bases in Ghazni and Paktika Provinces of eastern Afghanistan is honest to the point of harsh self-critique. You will see I have made no efforts to conceal our faults or vices, nor did I exaggerate the positive ways we supported each other through creativity and camaraderie. Our actions cast varying shades of gray in the continuum of right and wrong. If in the end you decide that these stories make us bad people, then chances are you never went to war.

PART 1:

DUDES OF WAR

THE CRUSADER

Forgive me Father, for I have sinned.

It's been three years since my last deployment.

During my combat tour in Afghanistan, I lied, stole, lusted, cheated, backstabbed, and killed. Some of these acts were natural and expected outcomes of my job as an infantryman. Some were the result of my on-the-spot command decisions, that overrode my normal moral sensibilities, in order to preserve the safety of my men, my mission, and myself.

And still others were unjustifiable acts of a tired man, a depressed man, a man looking for an easy way out. A man who never tucked his pant legs into his boots, whose uniform was adorned with unauthorized patches and was always ripe with sweat and dirt. A man on the edge of breaking down (over the edge at times, in fact), and who took shortcuts in order to ensure self-preservation. I had a mind that ran for days at a time on PTSD medications, and whose spirit ran on fumes and memories of the times when all my buddies here were still alive and had all their parts and pieces intact.

Simply put, there were long spells of time when I was a man who just needed to go hide in his hootch and hope the war would go away until I was ready to face it again. These delusional wishes never seemed to sway the enemy in eastern Afghanistan.

I was both a hero and a zero. A success story and a failure. I was the combat version of ying and yang. One moment I was being threatened with a negative counseling statement, and the next being awarded the Bronze Star. Given this dual persona, it's logical that I ended up with the duplicitous nickname Crusader by my teammate Spanky. It was meant both as a jab at my bleeding-heart hopes that I could single-handedly "fix" Afghanistan, and to positively acknowledge my dedication to trying to achieve these idealistic goals. I was the Elias character from the movie *Platoon*."Tupper," Spanky would say in his best imitation of Sgt. Barnes from the movie, "he's a crusader."

And so the nickname stuck, among many other nicknames I picked up over the year we spent in Afghanistan. Yeah, the Crusader was spot-on. It was the most accurate moniker for sure because I definitely did launch a couple crusades with my unit, which were not always well-received and not always successful. I taught myself beginner's Dari (the official language of Afghanistan), and took it upon myself to lobby our commander for the need for language classes for our unit. He had as much interest in this as he did converting to Islam and giving up beer and cigarettes. But to his credit, after incessant badgering, he agreed to a weekly hour-long class.

Suffice to say, Rome wasn't built in a day, and teaching someone an extremely difficult and confusing language like Dari can't happen in a couple hour-long sessions. But I gave it my all and I failed miserably. Most guys in my unit were too focused on the war-fighting part of the mission, and didn't see the benefits for having some rudimentary Dari language skills even though we would be embedded within the Afghan Security Forces. The groans that would come out of my buddies' throats when I would hand out homework or announce quizzes rivaled those of a seventh-grade classroom being told they had homework to do over summer vacation.

So while my crusade to teach infantry grunts a foreign language ended in a disastrous failure, I was able to launch another crusade that actually bore successful fruit.

I started an informal campaign to collect winter clothing and toys for local Afghans, which quickly snowballed into an international DIY (do-it-yourself) project that generated literally hundreds of large boxes of donated boots, shoes, clothing, and toys for impoverished villages in eastern Afghanistan. The boxes of items came at such a rate that they filled up my hootch, our supply room, and our storage sheds. We couldn't plan H.A. (humanitarian aid) missions fast enough to keep the donated inventory from overrunning our FOB.

Later, I was asked to brief my model of DIY humanitarian-aid collection and distribution to units deploying to Afghanistan who wanted to re-create its successes. The model showed small-scale units how to efficiently and safely collect and distribute aid without relying on slow bureaucratic supply chains of higher HQ. As a result of this simple "think outside the box," H.A. model of mine, the Crusader was able to vanquish the cold for literally thousands of Afghans, who received winter clothing, boots, and gloves for the first time in their lives.

War is a natural breeding ground for the idealistic actions of "crusaders" like me. But more often than not, it is also a fertile womb for acts contrary to the accepted moral standards of our culture, and I too found many ways to violate my well-established civilian world moral sensibilities in order to accomplish the mission and/or keep my sanity.

Perhaps the most disturbing part of this confession is that I never got in trouble for any of the actions I took that I knew were wrong. This made it all the easier to repeat them. And to complicate matters, many of the times that I was knowingly cutting against my own moral fiber was a direct result of being ordered to do it. That's not an excuse to ameliorate my culpability. I could have said no to my commanders when given an order I felt was either unethical or illegal. But that is easier said than done. It's just an uncomfortable truth that soldiers are regularly confronted with this dilemma to simultaneously follow orders that break their own personal moral rules, in order to fulfill higher goals. In war, the ends usually justify the means.

But it's not always this way. There were times that I refused to follow an order that for whatever reason was unwise or unethical. The irony is that these were the times I actually *did* get in trouble. Being a company-level officer means that when there is doubt about the wisdom of an order from higher, you are damned if you follow it and damned if you don't. That's pretty much how it goes at war where the proverbial rubber meets the road.

MR. OCD

The nickname is not a cheap-shot insult. He really does have OCD. And I think it's fair to say it made him a better soldier in a lot of ways. Even Mr. OCD would admit this to you once he got to know you and trusted you. It's not a confession that he gives out as a plea for help or an excuse for his shortcomings, but as a warning to what you could expect when working with him. Mr. OCD just doesn't want you to be the one who crosses the line and violates his myriad of OCD rules and regulations. He's got rank and a temper, so knowing how to avoid his pet peeves was a warning well-heeded to the soldiers around him.

I had a special place in Mr. OCD's world. I was his battle buddy. A battle buddy, in modern military parlance, is an informal assignment of mutual responsibility between two soldiers. If your battle buddy screws up, you screwed up. It's a custom the Army developed because it's less likely that two people get stuck on stupid at the same time. In other words, two minds are better than one.

The battle buddy system is mostly used in training environments, and seeing as we spent three months in a training environment before we were sent off to war in Afghanistan, bunking side by side in our communal hootch, I was able to master the art of screwing around with Mr. OCD's pet peeves without driving him over the edge. By the time we hit the combat zone, I had perfected the art of terrorizing my battle buddy. Add to this that I was equal to him in rank, I could get away with things that would put him into a violent rage if some enlisted Joe had perpetrated them.

The primary focus of Mr. OCD's anxiety centered around germs. A small bottle of hand sanitizer was always tucked into one of the many cargo pockets that adorned his ACU's (Army combat uniform). And the primary battlefield where he fought this war against microbes was his sleeping area in our hootch. The mere thought of someone touching his sheets or pillows was enough to make his voice tremble. He would return from his busy rounds securing gear and logistics for our unit, and we would taunt him with warnings that someone, while he was gone, had been messing around with his bed. He would smile, hoping to draw out an admission that we were just spinning a tall tale. But the ruffled bedding suggested our taunts were serious, and his brow would wrinkle as he began to sort out what had transpired in his absence.

In moments like these, more soldiers from our small specialized team would pile on, adding things like "Yeah, you should have seen what the Preacher did to your pillowcase. He got back from his PT run, stripped down naked, and rubbed his junk all over it." Truth be told, the Preacher would regularly return from his daily afternoon runs sporting a lather of sweat, which added a conditioned shine to his werewolf-like coat of body hair.

As he contemplated the idea of the Preacher's dark nest of wet, curly pubes rubbing on the same fabric he put his face to sleep on at night, the nervous smile would disappear from Mr. OCD's face. Now there was just rage mixed with fear that his bed had been fully compromised and overrun by another man's nut-sack sweat. More often than not, in these moments of complete emotional collapse, Mr. OCD would tear the pillowcase off his pillow and stuff it into a trash can before we could confess that the story was false.

Mr. OCD couldn't handle the thought of the act occurring, even if it hadn't, and his pillowcase would remain in the bin, sacrificed in order to clear his mind and allow him to drift off to sleep that night, cheek rested against a fresh, clean pillowcase whose honor had yet to be sullied.

Seeing as we were headed for a war zone in a country with little sanitation and a populace known for their lack of personal hygiene, I knew things were going to get rough for Mr. OCD. No supply of hand sanitizer would be a match for dust storms, local nationals, and the grime of sustained combat operations. Our taunts of the violation of his pillowcases would be pale in comparison to the real germ warfare he was about to experience.

To combat this, Mr. OCD carved out a small, clean private hootch on our FOB in Afghanistan that was meticulously maintained. He had the most organized wall locker and personal living space in the whole unit. In addition to an always-ready stack of new linens and pillowcases for his bed, it featured a wide range of personal hygiene and vanity items. Foods, beverages, and DVDs occupied one shelf, while his colossal collection of Skoal dip occupied another. Most dippers, including myself, had a couple spare cans of dip ready in a wall locker or rucksack. And even overseas in our corner of the war, we still were able to acquire, store, and have handy enough dip to get us through until the next resupply mission. But Mr. OCD brought his dipping habit to levels of hoarding unmatched by anyone in the U.S. Army.

Normally, his wall locker would remain padlocked (he correctly feared we would harass him by messing with his bedding and/or looting his goodies when he was not keeping a watchful eye on them). One day he let me into his hootch, and I asked if I could count his cans of dip. I stopped counting after one hundred. He had them organized by flavor (mint, peach, cherry, wintergreen, and straight), and then by cut: long, fine , and pouches. I hadn't arrived into his cove of cleanliness out of accident or boredom, and I was not counting his cans to pass the time. The fact was I was out of dip, and no convoys were lined up for days to go get more. I was tweaking from nicotine withdrawal, and needed to borrow some from Mr. OCD. But I knew if I revealed my difficult situation, he would pay me back for all my previous OCD-taunting mischief and toy with me like a cat does with a wounded mouse. I knew he would say no to my request to borrow a couple cans of dip.

I made a roundabout comment that he had way too many cans of dip, a supply that would clearly outlast the remaining months on our tour of duty. I said "I'll take a couple cans of peach off your hands." It was a flavor he had professed to hate. He said no. I should have known a good

logistician never gives anything away without getting something in return.

"I thought you hated peach." He agreed, but said if
we got our tour extended (as the current Army rumor du jour
circulating suggested), or if he increased his daily usage, he
would run out of his favorite flavors and be forced to use the
peach.

This was a bogus argument. He knew my dire situation, and he was playing hard to get but didn't want to come
right out and ask what I was willing to give him in return. I
had been outmaneuvered by Mr. OCD, and had no come-
back, nor did I have anything he wanted. I had no cash to
offer, so I was out of luck. I sat there frustrated, mouth water-
ing at the stacks of dip cans, jonesing for a nicotine fix, yet
helpless to do anything about it. Then, abruptly, Mr. OCD
was called away momentarily to answer a question from our
commander.

I stuffed a can of peach dip in my pocket and left. Score
one for the dirtbag.

The high-water mark of my good-natured harassment
of Mr. OCD occurred when he was away on leave. Accompanied by some teammates who had not tired of our game of
messing with his bedding, we gathered on the night before
he was scheduled to return to our FOB. We walked over to
his hootch with a camera, a teddy bear, and a five-star prank
ready to be put into play.

His hootch was co-located with the unit's tactical operations center (TOC) and we entered it while a high-level
meeting was underway between battalion and brigade staff.
We quietly walked past the assembled majors and lieutenant
colonels, pulled aside the blanket that served as OCD's door,
and entered his hooch. It was neatly organized as always,
awaiting the return of the perfectionist who called it home.
At the foot of his bed was an expensive and highly cherished
white sheepskin rug that he had acquired at a local bazaar. It
was one of his favorite items. I quietly stripped naked down
to my combat boots and laid myself upon it in a classic 1940s
pinup model pose, my junk firmly pressed into the soft wool

rug, and posed for a couple photos with a teddy bear he had given me earlier as a joke. My teammates were unsuccessfully holding in their giggles and guffaws as they snapped photos of the prank. We quickly exited his hootch, passing momentarily through the TOC where the meeting was still occurring. We walked past the battalion and brigade officers and exited. They stared dumbfounded as a half-naked man in combat boots, clutching a teddy bear, and others grasping cameras, left their meeting without an explanation for the visit.

The photos were then downloaded and printed out, and the next day, when Mr. OCD returned to his hootch, he was greeted by pictures of my bare ass taped up all over his walls, desk, and bed. When he saw them, he had to laugh to keep his head from exploding. The thought of his precious rug being defiled by my junk almost made him cry.

Mr. OCD's strength as an officer was in planning and supplying the rest of us on our missions outside the wire. He was perhaps the best logistical officer I've ever served with, and he was equally methodical on the occasion when he was given the reigns to plan and execute a mission. The three weeks that he had command of the unit (while our regular commander was on leave) were perhaps the most productive, well organized, and aggressive in regards to planning and executing missions. While his primary job description required him to stay on the FOB, he did pull some trigger time out on mission. And on one dreary day, he actually shot someone.

On this occasion we received the generic "be on the lookout for suicide bomber driving a white Toyota" warning order. For some reason, suicide drivers in Afghanistan were always driving a white Toyota. On the rare occasion it was a blue Toyota, but it was usually white and always a Toyota.

It was a simple traffic-control point mission, and given the extreme cold weather, it was pretty clear that Mr. OCD was not amused at being selected to leave his warm hootch to go out and play traffic cop in the sloppy, frozen mud.

So when a large, overly burdened commercial truck failed to heed the warnings of some frigid Afghan soldiers to stop at the checkpoint, Mr. OCD jumped from his Humvee and fired a few shots at the truck cabin. Fortunately for both parties, Mr. OCD was known for his logistical prowess more than his tactical skills. His shots pinged low into the trucks motor and radiator, but ricocheted into the cabin and hit the driver, causing painful but superficial wounds to his face and chest.

This event prompted an investigation into the shooting by higher. Had it happened to someone else, it would have probably been left alone as an unfortunate but necessary split-second decision. But Mr. OCD wasn't popular among the brass for previous germ-related outbursts against Afghans living and working on our FOB. And he had recently been called onto the carpet for a tirade against some Afghan inter-preters who were using the small exercise gym on the base. On this occasion, Mr. OCD launched into a scream fest filled with racially charged overtones, and fueled by his germ pho-bia, claimed the Afghans were dirty disease agents that had no place being in the gym. For added effect, he threw in the accusation that these Afghans were also thieves, responsible for the disappearance of everything he had lost or misplaced over the preceding months. Whether there was any evidence to support these charges is unclear, but it didn't go over well with the FOB commander.

Mr. OCD's legacy in Afghanistan, despite his hard work and commitment to the mission, was ultimately lessened by his idiosyncrasies and OCD anxieties. He worked longer and harder than most of us, but going to war in such a grimy and unhygienic place hampered his ability to earn the credit he was due.

Cropped for modesty, my infamous nude photo.

3

CASANOVA

Casanova was always able to make the best of a crappy situation. Like everyone else on our remote and rudimentary FOB, Casanova had gamed the system to procure extra goodies by bending rules here and there, with the end result of making his day-to-day life bearable, if not downright enjoyable. He was the first, as far as I could tell, to figure out how to procure alcohol and access (albeit virtual) to women back home in the States. But while booze and broads could be counted among his daily rituals, nicotine (the third member of the holy trinity of soldier religion) was not. Casanova was one of the few among us who didn't dip or smoke. He was truly the exception to the norm in this regard. Even the Afghan soldiers we worked with had a dip or smoking habit. In their case, the dip was a dreadful green powder made of god knows what, rumored to be laced with opium, called *naswar*. The smoke of choice for Afghan soldiers was hashish, locally grown and thoroughly enjoyed in their barracks pretty much every night.

I heard stories about some American soldiers on a large FOB in Kabul, who got busted for smoking hash in order to pass away the long twelve-hour shifts in their quiet part of the country. In our area, it wasn't something anyone seemed interested in trying, though a few guys braved a dip of *naswar*. This cross-cultural experiment ended abruptly when one U.S. soldier went into a coma from dipping *naswar* that had been laced with cyanide by a Taliban-sympathizing merchant.

Casanova avoided all the tobacco and smoke products on the market. Instead, he had a different sort of vice. He loved the ladies, and he loved the Internet, and he loved to enjoy both of them simultaneously with a cold beer after a long, stressful day out on a mission in Afghanistan. In the evenings he would prop himself up in his bed, like an old man settling in to watch his favorite TV sitcoms. With pillows fluffed, he would rest his laptop on his small pot belly, turn on a relaxing iTunes playlist, and log into the escapist Internet sub-universe of single women looking for a soldier boy to pleasure.

I mentioned that Casanova liked a cold beer in the evening. I should point out that drinking alcohol in Afghanistan is prohibited. Access to it for U.S. personnel is severely restricted, against regulation, and is very difficult to acquire, to say the least. Our NATO allies are permitted to drink, and the Afghan people don't seem to have a problem with it, but for whatever reason the gods at the Pentagon have declared it off limits for us while we are in country. The only authorized exception I ever saw to this rule was for the Jewish Passover, where bottles of wine were imported to the large FOBs for religious ceremonies. During this holiday, the ranks of soldiers claiming Jewish religious affiliation seemed to swell immensely, as word got out that wine was being served at their ceremonies. I even saw a Christian chaplain, apparently recently converted to the ways of the Hebrews, headed to the Passover table to get his share of the good stuff.

But at our FOB we had no Jews, and therefore had no wine, nor any legal access to alcohol. That meant that it either had to be smuggled into the country, or acquired through a third party—usually an Afghan interpreter or contractor who knew where to get it. Despite the fact that it's a Muslim country, whiskey and beer were behind the counter in most shops in the cities. Prohibition famously didn't work in the United States, and it's not working in Afghanistan either.

Casanova had a private cooler hidden under his bed, which was daily replenished with ice, and which served as the minibar for his evening nip. He had multiple women of interest, and would run chats simultaneously with different ladies. Some were hotties, some were train wrecks, but all were women, which is really all that mattered. On occasion I would hear him burst out with laughter as he pushed the envelope with triple-X messages to these women, and when we heard that distinctive chortle, we knew he had hit pay dirt. We would put down whatever we were doing and rush to his hootch. We would push aside the curtain he had hung over his doorway and barge in. He was kind enough to share his ladies with us, and would show us the explicit chat. Once in a while, he would even show us the naked pictures of the woman he was chatting with for a group show-and-tell.

If it was a woman he didn't have much interest in, he would take a piss break and pass his laptop off to another soldier and let them have fun writing racy messages to the unsuspecting woman. Do this. Touch that. Send me a picture. It was a great way to vent sexual tension, get some chuckles, and feel some connection—albeit dubious—to a living, breathing female back home. I never participated directly in this fun pastime, but I'm guilty of egging it on and of standing alongside my peers as they tried to outdo each other in perversion, suggesting new creative messages to send in the hope of raising the level of our jollies.

But this was not always a safe game to play and things got out of control when Casanova got a female cyber stalker. She was a rotund woman, pushing three hundred pounds easy (this was a conservative estimate, given the graphic pictures she sent him via e-mail). She was in love with him, and she e-mailed and texted him constantly. He would wake up in the morning to an inbox full of messages, ranging from pleas for love to threats if her love and devotion were not reciprocated. He wasn't interested in her at all, and no amount of friendly brush-offs seemed to deter her daily confessions of love. Because of this situation, Casanova got the nickname Chubby Chaser, and it took weeks of him ignoring her before she finally stopped IM'ing him.

Casanova wasn't alone in developing multiple female followers. We all were in various stages of breaking up with our girlfriends or getting divorced, and being tired of the single life in a womanless combat environment. None of us felt like it was wrong or cheating or abusive to engage in these virtual trysts. To the women in our lives back home, who thought they were the only ones receiving our affection and attention, they probably would have felt differently. But I would withhold judgment on the soldier in harm's way, longing to experience love in any form, spending a seemingly endless year in an environment devoid of females. We feared that every day would be our last, and doing whatever we could to feed the need for attention and affection from the fairer sex seemed like fair play.

So this Internet courtship continued as a daily ritual for many of us. Most of these Internet relationships were flashes in the pan. But some simmered for a while. Some chat sessions laid the groundwork for dates when we went back home on leave. Others evolved into long-term relationships and even marriage. Some guys ran a stable of women, almost as if they were in a game and got points for each score. Daily updates were given among the contestants to see how many women each had in play. Bonus points were given for super-hot girls or for a woman in an exotic location or far-off country. Mr. OCD had a woman in Scotland sending him triple-X pictures, and he felt that alone was grounds for him being declared the champion of the sport.

As high rolling as he thought he was, Mr. OCD was trumped by Gator, another member of our unit, who used the Internet to line up a trip to Thailand, where he spent his two weeks of leave rocking it 'Nam style with a twentysomething cute Thai girl and a rented motorcycle. When he came back to Afghanistan, we gave him a lot of shit for his escapade. We said it was really an underage boy he hired. We said he had raging VD now. We said all sorts of salty things, mostly out of jealousy for his success. He insisted that his conquest was not a prostitute, but was instead a "girlfriend" who he hired for the weekend from a bartender who had many to choose from. She cooked for him, washed his clothing, took a backseat on the motorcycle for joyrides across the Thai countryside, and perhaps most importantly, met his standards for sexual-performance needs with flying colors.

In the end, the joke was on Gator. He had met a woman on MySpace and truly fallen hook, line, and sinker for her. He had plans to come home to her, move in with her, and start a serious, perhaps lifelong relationship with her. I remember seeing him a few weeks before we came home, heading for the showers. He had the look of a lost puppy dog. I asked what was up, and he told me she had dumped him unceremoniously and without warning. He had gotten a Dear John e-mail, and was genuinely crushed by it all.

The Thailand and Scotland stories aside, the undisputed king of the long-distance dating game was Badger. Badger was young. He had swag. He had tats. He had abs. He had the classic good looks young ladies his age on the Net were interested in. These girls wanted to be with a heroic soldier out in harm's way, and Badger had an urgent desire to fulfill their wishes. This urgency was rooted in a fear that he wasn't going to survive his combat tour. He was candid about this before he went on leave, telling us he was going to live every day on leave like a god and spare no expense. He had that feeling in his gut that life was short and time was not on his side. His two-week leave was an almost religious quest to fulfill all his sexual fantasies, and visit all the big cities he wanted to see. He said he kept a book detailing the sex tricks, fetishes, and acts he wanted to experience before he died, and that he was going to check them off one by one, city by city. I never saw this book—it may itself have been a fantasy—but I wouldn't be surprised if it really did exist.

While in Afghanistan, Badger always had ladies lined up online. Some were past conquests. Others were future conquests who just didn't know it yet. When he arrived back in the States for leave, he emptied out his life savings from his bank account (he said it was about 10,000 dollars), and spent two weeks burning every cent on a coast-to-coast pleasure jaunt. He would fly from city to city (Denver and Las Vegas are the two I remember), rent an upscale hotel room, rent the most expensive car on the lot (usually a Cadillac Escalade), stock it with bottles of the finest bubbly, and to top off the experience, hire escorts who would help him check off some of the to-do items from the list in his book. Apparently, he made serious progress with his list during his two weeks at home on leave. Fortunately for us all, Badger's premonitions about dying in Afghanistan were erroneous, and he happily returned home at the end of his tour to an empty bank account.

We compared notes on which dating sites offered the best pool of women. There were pay sites and free sites, and those of us in the game checked them out for new profiles whenever we got the chance.

At the time, I was going through the first stages of separation and divorce, so I had an account on Match.com, and also a profile on MySpace that attracted a lot of soldier worshippers. It was flattering. It was addictive. It was a connection to women, which was something that had been completely severed by going to war in Afghanistan. Previous generations of young American boys had been sent to war in France and Vietnam and were surrounded by exotic women. Access was easy, be it the local brothels or the women truly interested in falling in love and leaving their war-torn countries for the easy life in America. But in our case, Afghanistan offered only an occasional peek at a woman enshrouded in the blue burkhas. The Internet, as dubious as it may have been, was our only contact with women. There were no women at all we interacted with face-to-face. There were no brothels. There were no serendipitous love affairs between soldiers and single female villagers. American soldiers on FOBs like ours were so deprived of contact with women, that they modified the familiar term "T & A" to refer to "toes and ankles" instead of "tits and ass." Toes and ankles were the only parts of women visible to us when we were out on patrols. I had never had anything resembling a foot fetish in my life, yet I developed an eye for toenail polish and high heels that rivaled my appreciation of cleavage and hip-hugging jeans back home.

The sun sets over the B-hut barracks that housed the hootches of Rainbow, Casanova, Fidel, and myself. The smaller building to the right housed our latrines.

4.

FIDEL

On every FOB in Afghanistan are people who wear the additional duty hat of the FOO. The FOO, or field ordering officer, is in charge of drawing a monthly lump sum of 25,000 dollars in Afghan currency and spending it on FOB improvements, emergency purchases, and other odds and ends to keep the American and Afghan Armies in fighting shape. In order to be the FOO, one has to complete a short course on the rules and regulations of FOO money, which usually occurs on the first couple days in country while you are in processing. Everyone in our small sixteen-man unit was required to attend this training, so we all got FOO certified and ultimately had experience dealing directly with FOO money and procedures.

FOO money comes with a lot of strings, regulatory dos and don'ts of things you are authorized to spend the money on and things you're not. On my first FOB in Ghazni Province, the guy who excelled the most at managing FOO money was Fidel. Fidel was a master of stretching every penny, as well as stretching the regulations relating to legal expenditures in order to get what was needed.

When we arrived on the FOB, we inherited an Afghan army base that had literally been left in tatters when the Russians abandoned it twenty years earlier. Wild dogs and homeless Afghans had moved in and called it home. Piles of dried human feces lined the corners of the rooms in the decaying buildings. Some were missing their entire roofs, long gone from windstorms and the scorching sun that had long since bleached the life out of Russian roofs. Dog skeletons were scattered across the ruined Russian airstrip, victims of forgotten mines and starvation.

American dollars quickly built some new small, wooden buildings called B-huts for our hootches, but these new living quarters were spartan at best in their decor and amenities. Every month, in part due to efficient FOO officers like Fidel, money was slowly but surely transforming this apocalyptic Russian disaster zone into a living facility more in tune with modern American standards.

When we got there, the kitchen consisted of a propane-fed gadget that had two stovetop burners. It weighted about ten pounds and could fit in a backpack, should one have wanted to move it. The propane tanks were refilled at the local Afghan sundry shop. Matches to light it came from Pakistan, and were as brittle as dried twigs. We would normally go through half a dozen before we could get the stovetop lit for boiling water.

We had a picnic-style table next to the mini-stove, a sink that got clogged frequently and drained into an open brown water pool just outside the kitchen wall, and a large freezer that held stacks of low-grade (but edible) frozen hamburger patties. It was pretty simple, and we supplemented this limited menu with food from the local economy, what we could beg, borrow, and steal from other U.S. bases, and what was mailed to us from home. My daily diet during the first weeks on the FOB was usually a can of tuna for lunch and a couple hamburger patties or a bag of ramen noodles for dinner. The result was an unfilled stomach in the evening and rock-hard dumps in the morning. I lost a lot of weight during the first months in country as a direct result of our rustic chow hall.

But through creative FOO regulation interpretation, and a commitment to radically improve our living standards, Fidel set out on an impressive campaign to remodel our kitchen and upgrade the palatability and enjoyment level of our diet.

Fidel was used to wheeling and dealing back home in the States. He was the guy who knew someone who knew someone and could get you anything you wanted anytime, anywhere. The fact that it may have been illegally secured was only a technicality. Fortunately for us, Fidel hadn't lost his love for the deal when he arrived in Afghanistan. In short order, and without anyone really noticing it, Fidel made contacts in the local community among a broad range of contractors, service providers, merchants, government authorities, criminals, and every other kind of character working the legal and black market economy in our area.

One day he gave me a peek into his connections in the Afghan black market as we drove to another U.S. base to pick up some supplies. He said he knew an American civilian contractor there who had direct ties to a mysterious and nefarious place in Pakistan known only as "Bush Avenue."

Bush Avenue, named after then President George W. Bush, was allegedly where millions of dollars of stolen and lost supplies ended up. Most of these goodies had been intended for U.S. forces in Afghanistan or were imports sent to fuel the materialistic needs of Indian and Chinese consumers. Once these items were diverted to Bush Avenue they weren't going to make it to their intended destinations. Name-brand electronics, furniture, foodstuffs, and clothing were rumored to be found there, and were quickly purchased by mid-level black marketers for redistribution to the four corners of the earth.

Fidel, with a coy smile on his face, asked me if I had any money I wanted to invest in some deals that he knew were on the table. His contractor buddy on the base where we were headed had recently been offered hundreds of Oakley Thump sunglasses/mp3 players allegedly from Bush Avenue, and he was looking for investors. The turnaround on the deal would be quick and the profits extreme. Fidel joked that it would be easy to use FOO money to fund these illegal purchases, get the original investment back quickly before anyone realized the money was gone, and make a large profit.

In hindsight, I wonder if he was joking. My hunch is that Fidel left Afghanistan a wealthy man far beyond the tax-free pay he earned from the Army. True or not, he liked to at least play up the idea he was a player among the businessmen of Bush Avenue.

Every Friday, jewelry and gem merchants would show up and hold a mini-bazaar on our FOB. As the weeks passed, the tradition seemed to fade away, as the merchants dwindled down to just one seller. But the slow death of the gem bazaar didn't occur because of a lack of interest among the soldiers. To the contrary, sales of gems and jewelry held steady during this period of time. I'm pretty sure the open bazaar faded away because Fidel had been working behind the scenes, negotiating with all the merchants to see who was willing to provide him the most patronage in order to have access to the FOB. The free market economy was dying a slow death in the grips of Fidel. He had mastered the common Afghan practice of monopolizing the marketplace through gifts, threats, and graft.

Eventually, there was just one jewelry merchant who showed up. The old bazaar had been set up next to our motor pool, and the vendors were restricted to that area. Now, with only one vendor involved, the rules had changed, and he had unrestricted access to the whole FOB.

The merchant, whose name I don't recall, was young, spoke decent English, and would make unannounced visits to our hootches. We would hear the common door to the B-hut open, then a lively Afghan voice would politely sing out, "Hello, it is me, selling wonderful jewelry for your girlfriend and wife!"

The funny thing about the last part of his greeting was that he meant it literally. He had been around so many soldiers on so many FOBS that he recognized that a piece of jewelry purchased for the wife was only half the potential sale. Too many soldiers had a girlfriend on the side, or multiple girlfriends, and this jewelry dealer was prepared to offer a helpful reminder that the "other woman" needed a little something too to keep her satisfied too. After all, in Afghan culture a man could have multiple wives, so why not try normalize this model of polygamy to Americans with spare cash to spend.

We would reply to the jeweler's presence with friendly retorts of "Chator-asti!" (Dari for "How are you?") or "come on in" or even a friendly "go fuck yourself!" if we weren't in the mood to be sold gems. Regardless of what you told the jeweler, though, he was going to try to make a sale, and we would see his well-manicured hands peel open our curtain door to our hootch, and a beaming face would peek in, grinning ear to ear. And there, cornering us in our hootch, he would pull out felt bags of loose gems, rings, and necklaces.

It was hard to get him out of your hootch until you agreed to buy something from him. I bought a couple items from him, but on subsequent visits, I would pretend I had to respond to an emergency call from the TOC (tactical operations center),running out of my hootch toward another B-hut in order to escape his heavy sales pitch.

One of the few side benefits of fighting a war in Afghanistan is that the country is truly awash in cheap and undervalued gems and jewelry for soldiers to purchase. Incredible deals are to be had at a fraction of the cost that you would pay back home, and I know at least a couple of soldiers who educated themselves on gemology during their tour, and made a fortune reselling high-quality stones once they returned home from the war.

Our friendly gem pusher was a likable enough guy, so we didn't toss him out on his head, even though some of us didn't like the regular violation of our private space. But one thing was sure: Whatever deal this lone merchant had made with Fidel to win exclusive access to our FOB, it was obviously very lucrative for both parties.

When Fidel's yearlong tour was over and he went home, I assumed some of his FOO duties, and the gem merchant made it a point to give me some free items the first time he saw me in the post-Fidel era. He wasn't being generous, he was being a smart businessman. He had no competition and he wanted me to keep it that way. His gifts were an unspoken contract to ensure he would have exclusive access to our FOB.

But before I was put in this prickly moral dilemma on determining the merchant's access to our FOB, I got orders and I was soon transferred to Paktika Province. I don't know what deals this merchant cut with the FOO who replaced me, but I'm sure it was on similar terms as those Fidel had established.

It would be unfair for me to leave Fidel's story here in these shady black market dealings, because the fact is that Fidel spent the vast majority of his time working hard on improving living conditions on our FOB. When our commander decided that the tiny, underdeveloped kitchen needed an urgent upgrade, it was no surprise that Fidel was appointed as the head guy on the project. He could stretch our FOO limited dollars and make miracles happen. Despite a small budget, he set his standards high, and with some help from Casanova and a couple other guys, a complete modern remodeling of the kitchen was planned.

None of us really had a grasp on how grand the kitchen plan was, because that's the way Fidel liked to operate, keeping others in the dark until it was too late to stop. Sharing too much information would result in too many questions. The less the commander asked, the better it was. The less the commander knew, the better it was.

Fidel's was such a grand plan that the ceiling of the existing kitchen literally had to be removed, and raised about three feet in order to house the new appliances he was ordering. While we were all expecting at best a budget upgrade, Fidel was building us an Afghan version of the Trump Towers.

To call the items he ordered "appliances" is an insult to the top-of-the-line restaurant-grade items we received. I figured we would get a common fridge and a regular stove, and that's about it. I couldn't for the life of me understand why they were raising the roof on the kitchen, as it was high enough for the items that were in there. But when a crane showed up to offload some oversized crates, I understood that we had not ordered anything remotely bordering on normal.

A gigantic warming unit (about nine feet tall, five feet wide, with about eight long warming shelves), and a commercial-sized fridge of equal size were carried in by four or five Afghans straining under the weight of the monstrosities. In fact, the appliances were so big that we left them unplugged for weeks because we didn't have enough food to fill them, nor the electrical capacity to run them.

The appliances had been shipped in through Pakistan, and I think originated somewhere in Europe. I've got a few friends in the restaurant business, and have been behind the scenes in a couple of their fancy restaurants, but to date I've never seen anything as impressive as the appliances we had in our dirty, remote FOB in Afghanistan.

I should add that a lack of proper chow-hall accommodations was the norm for soldiers training Afghan soldiers on their primitive FOBs at the time. When I headed for my second FOB in Paktika, I heard that they had an equally dismal chow-hall arrangement. When they arrived, there was no chow hall at all, as it had burned down. The Greek took it upon himself to be the unit chef and quickly created a field kitchen that, dare I say, served better chow than many of the Army mobile kitchens and Army-trained cooks provided.

Taking a page out of the Vietnam playbook, the Greek became a class-one "shit can" cook. He used old fifty-five-gallon oil drums, cut in half, to prepare food. In Vietnam, similar oil drums were used to burn human feces, thus the nickname. The Greek modeled these drums into an impressive barbeque operation. Every night the Greek would serve steaks that he had marinated, tenderized, and prepped during the day. It wasn't the healthiest of diets, but we could at least look forward to the sweet smell and taste of good meat on the grill prepared by an excellent, motivated cook.

By the end of his tour, despite his impressive kitchen overhaul, Fidel had completely fallen out of favor with our commander. Some of his shortcuts and questionable decisions caught up with him, and he was facing formal negative counseling for some of these personal and professional indiscretions. He became isolated and the stress really started to tear him apart. He was put on a myriad of medicines for stomach ulcers and PTSD-related problems of sleep, depression, and anxiety. In the early days, I would hear him singing spontaneous silly songs in his hootch, incorporating us into the comical lyrics. By the end, his comical and upbeat personality had been replaced by that of an angry, paranoid man who whispered rants to himself in the semi-privacy of his hootch.

Cranes were required to unload the giant kitchen appliances from an eighteen-wheeler flatbed truck.

The large shipping crates containing the appliances were too large to fit in the existing kitchen, so the roof was removed and raised.

The kitchen was completely remodeled by Afghan contractors to make room for the new sink, stove, and oversized appliances.

The completed, remodeled kitchen, thanks to Fidel, FOO funds, and the unsuspecting generosity of the American taxpayer.

5

OLD YELLER

I f you thought the Army's use of mules ended in 1956, when the last government mules were formally deactivated and released from service, you would be wrong. The 130-year history of mules in the military formally ended in December of that year, but no one seems to have told Old Yeller.

Mules had served in every war the U.S. Army fought up to Korea. Old Yeller started his military career a few years later, and served in Vietnam, Iraq, and now Afghanistan. He wore a First Cavalry combat patch, and we often joked that he'd earned it on top of a horse like the old-time cavalry used to ride out west in the Indian wars (for those not acquainted with the venerable First Cavalry patch, it features a large horse's head).

Old Yeller was a man who loved mules. He was a simple, honest old coot. With his heavy Texas accent, he'd mumble his way through conversations about mules in the same way the character Taggart in the movie *Blazing Saddles* would talk about life in the southwest. In one scene from *Blazing Saddles*, Taggart is formulating a plan that involves the threat of violence, and explains *"That's where we go a-ridin' into town, a-whompin' and a-whumpin' every livin' thing that moves within an inch of its life. Except the womenfolks, of course."* These words echoed in tone and spirit the kind of thing Old Yeller would say before a mission into a Taliban-controlled area. Old Yeller was the epitome of the old mule-driving cook from any cowboy movie you've ever seen.

Old Yeller had spent a good number of years on the combat chuckwagon circuit, and it's fair to say he was a little past his prime in the art of war. To his credit, he was still an ardent patriot who didn't want to hang up his spurs, and he still had something in the gas tank to offer. But everyone eventually hits a wall and needs to pass the torch along to the next generation. In my time with him on our FOB, Old Yeller had a few age-related run-ins with the commander over mistakes made during missions. The most celebrated, embarrassing, and outright scary was when Old Yeller accidentally fired a 40mm grenade from a Mark 19 grenade launcher into the heart of the city surrounding our FOB. While trying to clear the Mark 19 one night after returning from a mission, the weapon accidentally discharged. The 40mm grenade round makes a funny Nerf-toy *poof* sound as it leaves the barrel, which is followed by silence as the egg-shaped grenade slowly flies in its casual arc toward its target. Everyone cringed upon hearing this *poof* noise, knowing that Old Yeller had just screwed up royally. The silence was eventually broken by a far-off, muffled explosion as the grenade impacted on some unseen and anonymous street in the dark city. This accident was ultimately labeled a "negligent discharge" by our chain of command, and the incident caused a major fuss at the FOB among our small unit, splitting those who felt it was an innocent mistake that any fatigued soldier could make after a long day's mission, and those who thought it was a sign that Old Yeller was past his prime for combat activities.

This set Old Yeller off on a path of frustration, and led him to wage a passive protest against what he felt was an unjust persecution due to an honest mistake, that frankly, anyone in the same situation (in the dark, after a long mission bouncing around in the gun turret, hungry, fatigued) could have made. But 99 percent of us don't make that mistake, so some sort of punishment was inevitable.

The next morning Casanova went to the city's hospital to see if anyone had been admitted the night before with frag or blast wounds from the 40mm grenade, and fortunately no one had. Apparently the round landed harmlessly on some dusty, unoccupied corner. Old Yeller didn't have to add the burden of guilt for harming someone to his already bruised ego. But he did have to shoulder the weight of a formal negative counseling statement from his boss.

It seemed like this event really put a damper on Old Yeller's whole tour, and he slowly disengaged himself from being a proactive teammate. Griping became his new number-one hobby, second only to his continued fascination with all things mule.

I mentioned at the start that Old Yeller had a fascination and love for anything mule-related, and that he kept the tradition of the Army mule alive in Afghanistan by living, breathing, and dreaming anything and everything mule-related. While most of us were online trying to line up women to rendezvous with when home on leave, Old Yeller was online visiting mule Web sites and shopping for mule-related gear on eBay. He received regular mule-trader magazines and newsletters, and I must admit, he educated me on a subculture I didn't know existed in the modern era. Apparently, there are lots of people out there whose dream vacation is to pack up a chuck wagon, stick a mule or two in the front of it, and ride off into the southwest pretending that it's 1860.

And fortunately for Old Yeller, Afghanistan was able to provide him with constant stimuli for his mule love. People in rural areas still rely on these beasts of burden for transportation and agricultural work, so there was often a donkey or mule that would cross our path out on mission. Many were the times that Old Yeller would pull the convoy to a halt, hop out, and pet a donkey. If time permitted, a photo was taken, or even a quick ride was given. If there was a donkey or mule within a mile of our location, Old Yeller was gonna find it.

6

SHRAPNEL

A lot of us liked chew tobacco, but nobody in our small sixteen-man unit could hold a candle to the man called Shrapnel. Shrapnel was a god among men in the tobacco-chewing pantheon, with an iron lip and equally tough gums that withstood constant assaults of wintergreen long cut dip. From morning to nightfall, you would find him with a fat bump of Grizzly wintergreen dip protruding from his lower lip.

His nickname Shrapnel had nothing to with his infantry duty assignment, nor did it refer to the lethal shards of grenades and mortars as they exploded and tore through the flesh and bone of the men around him in combat. Instead, it referred to a much more mundane reality of his life at war: His obsessive consumption of dip. The huge bump in his lip was so omnipresent that even the Afghans picked up on it. Unlike all the other nicknames my unit members picked up along the way, his was the only one that came from the Afghans themselves. Apparently, *shrapnel* is among the vocabulary list of words learned by Afghan interpreters in the course of their English-language instruction, and they were able to properly apply it metaphorically to our American teammate. It happened one uneventful day when Janis (one of our male combat interpreters) came into the TOC to complain about something new that Shrapnel had done to offend their Afghan sensibilities, and in a fit of rage, Janis blurted out, "We will quit if we have to work any more with Shrapnel!"

The Americans assembled in the TOC had never heard this nickname used before to refer to our dear comrade, and we all busted out laughing at the remark. Indeed, his lower lip and mouth area always looked like an explosion had just occurred. Small shreds of tobacco sprayed outward like the aftermath of a suicide bomber, and stuck to everything in sight when he talked in his deep south Arkansas accent. The corners of his mouth had permanent stains of crusty brown spit, and flecks of dip would fly out at you like shrapnel when he got excited and talked too fast. From that moment on, the nickname stuck.

Shrapnel had come to our FOB after a series of unsuccessful previous placements in other units and other locations. He was the puppy that would get adopted, only to be returned to the pound for biting someone. He'd spent only a couple weeks out with Lancelot at FOB Tillman on the Pakistani border, before the commander there saw it was a bad mix. The area of operations was too tough and required a zero-defect soldier. And given what had happened to Lancelot's battle buddy who was a stud among men (he was killed in action), even being a superman wasn't enough to guarantee survival.

Before his short stay at FOB Tillman, Shrapnel had previously been at another FOB, where he had also been transferred as a problem child. I don't know how to say this diplomatically, but many of us thought he had a screw or two loose. Don't get me wrong, he was a very friendly guy, honest, a team player, and an American hero who had volunteered to come do this difficult work. But at times, he would just say and do things that begged the question, "Is this dude retarded?"

We all did a few dumb things over there, but Shrapnel's foibles ticked off like clockwork. In situations where the outcome was critical to mission success, there was a 50-50 chance he would put the proverbial foot in his mouth and put someone at an unacceptable risk. And in an unforgiving combat environment, this was unforgivable.

Ironically, despite his dislike and mistrust of Shrapnel, it was Janis who one day saved his life. If memory serves me correctly, it was before the organized interpreter boycott against working with Shrapnel, and was likely one of the last straws that led them to that dramatic decision. During Operation Mountain Fury, a huge, coordinated offensive along the eastern portion of the country, Janis and Shrapnel got into a firefight with a squad of Taliban. Shrapnel was with an

Afghan soldier named Ali and had pushed too far forward of friendly lines. Janis, being the overall super dude that he was, decided to stay with them so as to not let them get surrounded. Ali was a firebrand leader, brave to the point of suicidal, and Shrapnel was following Ali's lone charge into the fray with Janis behind him. Ali jumped over a wall and was quickly killed by a rotund Taliban positioned to his front. As Janis recounted to me, Shrapnel then decided it was a good idea to jump over the same wall and see if he could have better luck. He hopped over, and fortunately for him, stumbled to the ground in a heap of body armor and gear. Janis quickly propped himself up against the wall and gave him covering fire, shooting the rotund Taliban soldier dead before the adversary could get a bead on Shrapnel. It was reckless moves like jumping over the wall that didn't win you favor among the men who would have to risk their lives to pull your nuts out of the fire.

Again, I need to say I don't want to sound like I'm piling on Shrapnel. *We all made mistakes like this in combat.* But those of us who survived learned from such a mistake and never did it again. Shrapnel didn't seem to gain wisdom from these teachable moments. And it didn't make it any better that at times, his lack of common sense put others in danger.

I recall vividly a couple days after Ali was killed, while out on mission, Janis and another interpreter named Noori running over to my Humvee with sweat pouring from their sweaty, dust-caked foreheads. They were in a fit of rage of such intensity that they were sputtering out their words. "Shrapnel has left us! He left us to die and be captured by the Taliban!" shrieked Janis. Noori was just as agitated, choking back tears and breathing heavily. Janis was a tall, handsome young interpreter, who spoke softly and politely under even the tensest situations. In months of working with him, I had never seen him raise his voice, so I knew his angst was legitimate.

I tried to calm the interpreters down, and asked them what had happened. Shrapnel's Humvee had been co-located with us outside a village for the last hour, and I knew

Shrapnel had no ill-will towards these interpreters to cause him to want Janis and Noori to get captured. Shrapnel didn't have a mean bone in his body.

I turned to Casanova, who was up in the gun turret of our Humvee, and said, "I don't know what the fuck they are yelling about, but I'm sure if it involves Shrapnel, it's gonna be interesting." Janis regained his composure, and explained that he and Noori had been given the word that Shrapnel's squad, which he was assigned to, was leaving the area to go to another village soon, and to be ready to move out. He and Noori had been riding in Shrapnel's Humvee for the mission, so they wandered off a short distance to piss and get some Afghan food, and returned to the Humvee's location within the specified window of time, only to see a fading dust cloud as Shrapnel's squad's vehicles disappeared into the valley below. Even after Janis's story provided a cooldown period, Noori still was so upset that he couldn't talk. It looked like he was either about to cry or vomit.

Janis was slowly working out his rage as he told me this tale, and his tantrum reminded me of newsreels I had seen of Benito Mussolini giving speeches to a passionate crowd of followers. Janis stomped his feet and waved his finger in the air like Il Duce as he cussed out Shrapnel in a jumbled mix of English and Dari. Janis was yelling up to the heavens, and had Allah or Muhammad been listening, we would have seen a lightening bolt strike Shrapnel's Humvee and blast it into pieces off in the distance.

After he finally finished his rant, I told Janis to chill out, grab a seat on the dirt, and I would call Shrapnel on the radio and get him to turn around and come back to pick them up.

I made contact with Shrapnel on the radio, and I could tell by the tone of his voice that he was in his classic happy-go-lucky lighthearted mood. I asked him why he had left Janis and Noori behind. He replied that he didn't know what I was talking about, as the interpreters were presently sitting behind him in the backseat of his Humvee. Confused, I asked him to take a peek in the backseat and tell me who was there.

A moment passed. The radio went silent as he realized his error and was quickly trying to come up with an explanation to explain away his faux pas. The pregnant pause passed, and his voice came back on the net and shot out through my radio speaker. "Uh, roger that, I guess we forgot to check to see if the interpreters were on board, we are turning around to come get them now". He was chuckling as he spoke. Over hearing this response, Janis and Noori's blood pressure rose back up to heart attack levels. Off in the distance, we watched as the Humvees and Afghan Army pickup trucks slowly curved around the dusty plain and headed back in our direction.

He forgot to check? This was the kind of nightmare innocent mistake that cost men their lives at war. Had we left before his unit, there would have been no one for Janis and Noori to run to. There would have been two unarmed combat interpreters, in U.S. military uniforms, left to fend alone for themselves in a Taliban-infested area. Of course, Shrapnel would have eventually realized they were missing at some point down the road and turned back to this village. He likely would have found the two interpreters casually seated in the village square, with their unattached heads in their laps and a note pinned to their chests decrying the infidels and the collaborationist Afghans (read: interpreters) who supported them.

This was the kind of mistake that was unacceptable. This was the kind of mistake that got officers relieved of duty and sent to some desk job in the rear. It was the kind of mistake that Shrapnel seemed to always have at the ready, and this was the reason why most of the interpreters threatened to quit their jobs when they were assigned to him. This was why Shrapnel had been passed on from FOB to FOB, because no commander wanted to have to eat the shit sandwich that Shrapnel was occasionally in the kitchen putting together.

Janis, the combat interpreter, in a calmer moment, and Ski in the background, never missing a chance to flash the "shocker" hand signal.

7

JACOB

The first thing I did when I heard Jacob had been severely wounded in combat was go steal his dip. He kept his Skoal long cut wintergreen tins in the communal fridge in the TOC , among the Gatorades and Red Bulls and bottled water from Kuwait. It seemed a strange place to keep his dip, given that none of us kept ours refrigerated, nor accessible to the sticky fingers of fellow nicotine addicts.

It must have been a Midwestern thing (trusting your neighbors with your stash), because none of us Northeasterners dared to leave our dip out in the open like that. It was just too easy to steal it from the communal fridge. No one else risked caching their dip outside of the safety of their own quarters. Given the wide range of nicotine addicts constantly wandering our FOB looking for a "bump," it was shocking that no one had stolen it before me.

It was an unwritten code among soldiers that you never steal your brother's stuff from their private hootch. But leaving things unattended in a communal area was tantamount to hanging a *FREE* sign above it.

Either way his Skoal dip had been unmolested in our communal fridge up until the moment I heard he had been hit by an RPG and was on his way to Germany for surgeries to reattach his leg.

So as I sat in the TOC and listened to other soldiers who had been with him recount what happened when they got hit by a Taliban ambush, I slinked over to the fridge, reached in, and pulled out the remaining cans of his Skoal dip. If I didn't take it, someone else would have. I was just the first guy to remember that it was there, on the bottom shelf next to the Red Bulls. Score one for situational awareness.

I then sat down at the large wooden table in the TOC's main meeting room, with my stash of Skoal tins safely lodged in my newly bulging pant's cargo pockets, and began to clean the carbon-choked weapons left over from the battle that nearly took Jacob's life. It was a team effort to get all the weapons cleaned up and in working order. It was the first thing we did when we returned from a gunfight. The crew-served weapons, once cleaned, would go back on the truck. The small arms would be hung back up in our hootches. But given the severity of his wounds, Jacob's weapons would be shipped back to the rear, and then Stateside to be returned to his home unit, which technically owned them.

The next day I made a visit to his hootch. As I entered it, I paused to remember a popular T-shirt I had seen some Army Rangers wearing back in the day. I had seen them on an active duty post down south, where my National Guard unit was stationed for two weeks of summer training. On the front of the shirt was a silhouette of a muscular soldier carrying a fallen comrade, slung over his shoulder in the firemen's carry. On the back, in big black letters, it simply said *IF YOU DIE, WE ARE SPLITTING UP YOUR GEAR.*

It was the kind of T-shirt that made us part-time week-end warriors envious of the real studs of war. We were jealous that we would never be able to experience such glorified moments of manhood. But now, entering Jacob's empty hootch, months into my tour in hell (better known as Ghazni Province, Afghanistan), I wasn't the only one who had been reminded of that old infantry slogan. Other guys from my team had already been there, selecting and taking needed items that Jacob would no longer require. To be clear, none of us took any big-ticket items that would screw over the government or Jacob's accounting of property he had been officially issued, but we rummaged through the odds and ends of his personal high-speed gear and snatched up things he would no longer need, what with his leg being re-attached in multiple surgeries in Germany.

We were living on a remote FOB, so it was kind of expected that people would take stuff we needed. I took Jacob's rigger belt to replace the belt I had, which was torn and broken.

Sure I stole it.

Giddy-up.

But without sounding overly sentimental, I'll confess that part of my looting of Jacob's gear was out of a desire to have a memento, something with me that I could keep to remind me of the soldier who would never return. It would be my piece of a man who could have and should have been a good friend, but thanks to the Taliban, instead was taken away after only a few short weeks in Ghazni. He was a man who I barely got to know, and who I have had little to no contact with since that eventful day. It's too bad, because Jacob was one of those guys you could have in your circle of friends for life. But instead I only knew him for a month, and then it was all over.

I still wear that belt today.

So while Jacob was recovering in a hospital somewhere in Germany, most likely staring at nurses' asses, we sniffed around the piles of gear in his hootch. There was a minor scuffle between a couple of guys over his impressive stack of porno DVDs. In the end they were divvied up equitably among the competing parties.

The next day news from higher made it official. Fidel and I got orders from Deathwish to formally prepare the paperwork and inventory and package up his remaining gear to be sent home. We went into his hootch with clipboards and garbage bags and began neatly folding his uniforms and clothing. We packed everything in plastic bags, which then were stuffed into sturdy cargo chests. We threw away a bloody uniform and various half-used personal hygiene items. His hootch was then swept and cleaned and made ready for his replacement, who would be arriving in the coming weeks.

8

DEXTER

The standard Army combat tour in Afghanistan is twelve months long. In Army jargon, it was known as a year of "boots on the ground." Once our tour started, we didn't waste any time in beginning to count down the days until it was over. A pinup girl wall calendar, with thick smudged pencil strokes forming X's that crossed off the days to measure time, was our fathers' way of measuring how "short" they were in 'Nam and Korea.

But today, this wall calendar has been replaced by computer programs that greet us every time we crack open our laptops and PDAs. It's right there on our computer's desktop, ticking off the seconds like a faithful soldier pulling guard watch, never missing a beat. At any given time during the year, with a quick glance at our laptop—which everyone had—we could get an exact measure of how many seconds, minutes, hours, and days remained until we would be going home to a cold beer and a hot girlfriend, or wife, or in some cases, both.

On every level, today's war is high tech, even in a backwards country like Afghanistan. And the king of high-tech gadgetry in our unit was Dexter.

Dexter's hootch was more like a NASA command center. He took a twelve-by-twelve windowless concrete hootch and turned in into a global communication center, movie theater, arcade, and nerve center for logistical operations. The countdown clock on his laptop had a myriad of data, all measuring the steady march of time remaining until he could go home. The lower corner displayed a traditional pie graph (the red slice was remaining time and the blue slice was expired time). It also showed the countdown in terms of seconds, hours, days, weeks, and months. It was constantly updating itself; fractions and numbers all moving in the right direction. Each tic-tock of the clock on his countdown timer was a step toward home.

Dexter wasn't the only guy obsessively checking his countdown timer. We all had a version of this simple computer program keeping track for us. Checking the timer was a habit as common as checking the weather or the close of the New York Stock Exchange. It was a dependable ritual in a land of unpredictability. It was therapy for all of us to sit and stare at our laptop screens at night, and watch the seconds pass from the column of war and death and fear, to the column of home and family and beer and sex. And unlike the war, it was the one thing we could count on everyday to always be going in the right direction.

We are the first generation of soldiers to be tied into this hi-tech war lifestyle. Our needs are no different from our forefathers, but our experiences make our stories of war unrecognizable to those who fought before us. From our little hellhole FOB, we passed the days out on mission in real-world combat. Then for a nightcap we shot up more bad guys on the Xbox playing Modern Warfare. If the Wi-Fi was working, we could even do it from the comfort of our individual hootches, remotely fighting against other soldiers bunked down for the evening on the other side of the barracks.

Dexter purchased a screen projector on eBay and rigged up a large movie screen on a sheet that hung on the wall. He scrounged up couches and comfy chairs from God-knows-where, and set a schedule for the movies and TV shows in his extensive DVD collection. We watched all sorts of miniseries from start to finish, usually HBO products like *The Office* (the British version), and *Deadwood*. New movies that were still in theaters back in the USA had already arrived on bootleg copies in the bazaars in Afghanistan, so we could watch grainy copies of the hot Hollywood releases any night of the week.

Dexter had also been kind enough to set up a Skype account that we could use. It was a real U.S. phone number with an answering machine he brought from home to capture any calls we missed while out on mission. Had you called one of us on that number, you would have thought you were talking to your neighbor down the street. It was running through one of the numerous laptops he was constantly using to keep us connected with the real world. He also had fridges, music, and a wide assortment of video games there for his teammates to use and share. Day or night, Dexter's laboratory was the place to go.

Places like Dexter's hootch radically changed our relationship with the home front. The limitations of entertainment and global communication had been erased. The infrequent mail call of previous wars has been replaced by text messaging, Internet dating, social networking pages, and Webcam sex with the wife, girlfriend, or both. Why write a letter home about the day's events when you can Twitter it instantaneously from the battlefield or call in an action-filled report to the home front on Skype. The Dear John letter has been replaced by an instant text message, which can arrive in real time in the middle of a gunfight on a dusty village road. Your love life now comes to war with you, instantaneously accessible and intruding, yet limited to a virtual level that teases and frustrates more than it satisfies.

Our high-tech era makes for an interesting war experience, to say the least. It helps us forge many new relationships, tears down others, and provides for a nice distraction from the grisly and terrifying business at hand. And thanks to guys like Dexter, it was available for the low-tech guys like me who couldn't figure out how to plug in a wireless router, let alone make it work.

9

THE GREEK

Remember back in high school, when the cool kids had the designer threads and the poor kids wore cheap clothing? The newest, flashiest brand-name stuff was a badge of social prowess, and the more you had, the easier it was to climb up the ranks into the realm of popularity.

Not much has changed since then, and judging by what I see today in the Army, a race to sport the newest, coolest gear, just like high school, is constantly underway with a full head of steam. We as soldiers are all contestants in the hunt for the new serviceable and tactically fashionable item. In Army lingo, the guys who personify this never-ending pursuit of new stuff are known as Geardos (a fusion of the words *gear* and *weirdos*). In my unit, I jokingly called our Geardos' endless pursuit of new tactical stuff the "arms race," and the term stuck and became a running joke, especially with the undisputed leader in this gear arms race: an NCO known as the Greek.

The arms race began the first week we arrived at our mobilization training down in Camp Shelby, Mississippi, and it didn't stop until we all left Bagram Air Base a year later.

The first shots in the Geardo war occurred when a UPS box addressed to the Greek arrived at our communal hootch during the first week of mobilization training. And the shots continued well into our tour, with more UPS and FedEx and DHL boxes arriving months later when we were living in our remote and distant FOBs in the mountains of eastern Afghanistan. These bundles of Geardo joy delivered the newest military items to the Greek, as well as other competing unit members, who were constantly fighting to be the leader in the arms race.

Given the proliferation of small designer companies pumping out new and improved tactical gear, it's not a surprise that Uncle Sam's official government-issued items just couldn't keep up with the evolution of gadgetry. Woe is the soldier who had only the items he was issued by Uncle Sam: It was tantamount to the poor kids wearing the Kmart sneakers and Rescue Mission hand-me-downs in high school.

The efforts one made to be the best Geardo were intense. Money was no issue. To be perceived to be at the vanguard of the new-gear arms race was worth every penny. And in this regard, the Greek had a big financial advantage in funding his arsenal. His wife had recently won a sizable chunk of money in the lottery, so he had more slack than the rest of us to spend money on tactical accessories.

The arms race involved a predictable and regular sequence of events. First, someone, usually the Greek or his next closest rival, Spanky, would order a new accessory. Second, the ritual of its arrival and introduction to the unit would be a celebrated event witnessed by all. The recipient would open the box to a crowd of anxious and jealous onlookers. We would stand around and ogle the new item, enviously wishing we had found it first.

In the following days, familiar packages from UPS, FedEx, and DHL would arrive bearing the same item, but for other soldiers, all trying desperately to keep pace in the arms race. The delivery trucks kept up a frenzied pace bringing us bipods, tripods, slings, chest rigs, optical sights, magpul ammo grips, and mini-flashlights, all of which passed through the threshold of our communal hootch.

The list of privately purchased gear went on and on. The thing is, once an item became too popular and common among the unit, it no longer had any pizzazz and a new one had to be acquired by the arms race leader to maintain the desired level of prowess and tactical street cred.

One would think that the hunger for new gear would eventually be satiated. But in fact, once an item became commonly purchased and owned, it entered another level of competition. Case in point: the bipod.

The Falcon was the first to buy a high-speed bipod for his M-4 rifle. We weren't issued any bipods by Uncle Sam, so this was an arms race coup. Soon many soldiers in the unit had purchased the same thing. But at this point, the bipod had lost its uniqueness and was common among the troops, so someone had to up the ante. The Greek declared that the standard black color of the bipod was not tactically correct enough, and a can of sand-colored spray paint was purchased to correct this flaw. With the application of spray paint, the arms race had entered a whole new level of competition.

Before long, our hootch was billowing with toxic spray-paint fumes, as soldiers were busy painting their gear in variations of sand and brown and green. It was a whole new battlefront that had been opened up in the gear arms race. Color was now adding additional points to one's efforts, making scoring the front-runner in the arms race even more difficult.

Classic olive drab green tones were frowned upon, as they were so 1980s. Everyone knew Afghanistan had nothing green, so only a fool who wanted to attract enemy fire would sport it. Brown was generally seen as an acceptable color selection, as it was agreed that it was a color that could blend into many the Afghan landscapes we had seen on TV and in magazine photos.

But a sand tone was the undisputed best choice of spray paint to use, given the desertlike terrain we expected to be operating in. Eventually, the sand colors won out, and it was hard to find any items that remained green or brown. Yet just when the paint fumes had cleared, and we thought we had reached some equilibrium in the pursuit for the most tactical gear, another layer of competition evolved: Should the spray paint be matte flat, satin, or semigloss? Those who had finally gotten on board with the earthy sand paint color schemes, but had bought semigloss paint, lost points on their gear color-customization projects. It was determined by the body politic of our unit that even the most inexperienced private knew that shiny accessories would only attract the eye of the enemy on the field of battle.

In the heat of the absurdity of the gear arms race, I began to develop fake products in an attempt to show my buddies how silly the tit-for-tat purchases and modifications were becoming. The fact was everything we were issued by Uncle Sam was better than anything our enemy would have, and it had all been rigorously field tested before being issued to us. To make my point, I reached into the stratosphere of hyperbole and sarcasm and created a fictional uber-tactical gear catalog that was, through comedy, an attempt to show people the absurdity of their never-ending hunt for the perfect product.

Using my slightly-above-average art skills, I put together two fake catalogues of gear, one originating from the Greek's fictional company and one from that of his biggest rival in the arms race, Spanky. The catalogs became popular daily reading for my unit as the amusement they provided helped to pass the three-hour-long training classes we were enduring in the 100-plus-degree Mississippi heat.

Every couple days I would introduce more products from the fictional catalogs, and they would be passed around discreetly during these classes to keep my buddies from going stir-crazy. Some of the fictional items included a tactical spittoon that was worn like a camelback canteen, a field manual on the methods of tactically jerking off in a combat environment, day vision goggles, and my favorite: the R.A.N.G.E.R., which was spawned by a guy in our unit, nicknamed Ranger, who had a proclivity for either losing gear or misplacing it. The R.A.N.G.E.R stood for "Rugged, Any purpose, Nug approved , Gear and Equipment Retainers." The product was a ten-cent piece of 550 cord (rope) that you would tie onto your item and then tie the other end to your belt. I had turned the classic Army "dummy cord" into a high-priced essential piece of tactical gear for the low cost of $99.99. Fortunately for my unit members' bank accounts, these items weren't really for sale, because I'm sure someone would have wasted their money on a couple of my creations in the endless hunt for the newest piece of high-speed designer gear.

Perhaps the best real-world example of the folly of the gear arms race was the hunt for the perfect holster. Uncle Sam issued us a thigh rig that allowed for the low-hung placement of our M-9 Beretta pistol on our leg just above the knee.

The cool kids, led by the Greek and his arch-rival Spanky, decided that this was a horrible design concept, and many a thigh rig were tossed and replaced with a private-purchase holster that placed the weapon further up the leg and nearer to the waist.

I remember Ranger spending hours debating which holster he should buy. He treated it like a major purchase, like a house or a new car. It was serious business with life-or-death consequences in his mind, and he eventually settled for an expensive holster that set off a pursuit among others for an even better holster.

Like the historically rising hemlines on women's skirts, the fashion worthiness of holsters began to be measured by how high up they rode on the wearer. Within weeks, pistols were practically invisible under the body armor we wore. A thigh rig was so passé. Wearing anything low was considered tantamount to tactical and fashion suicide.

Yet when all was said and done, after our yearlong tour at war was over, not one of us had ever fired our M-9 pistol in combat. The arms race for the perfect high-speed gunslinger holster was all for naught.

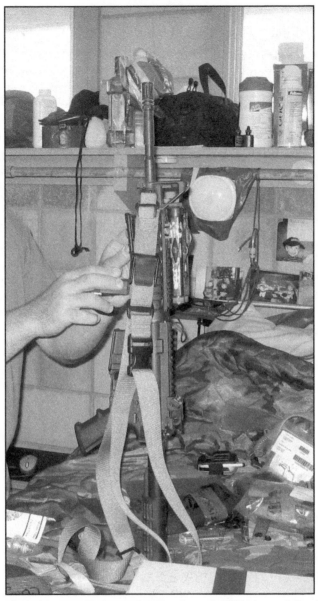

Caption: A soldier proudly shows off a privately purchased high-speed sling for his M-4 rifle.

THE FALCON

Sometimes we let our cockiness slip into arrogance. Sometimes we are so busy throwing others under the bus that we fail to see our own shortcomings. When it comes to forging a team, and completing missions with a unified esprit de corps, this holier-than-thou attitude makes us our own worst enemy. In war—and frankly, in all things in life—I think everyone is at one moment or another guilty of these ego-driven crimes. Be it myself, Mr. OCD, Badger; the list is long. We all fell into this trap at times. But perhaps the most frustrating personal display of these tendencies came from a soldier called the Falcon.

The Falcon had so much to offer as an experienced and wise soldier, and he had a charismatic, chipper attitude that drew people to him. He had natural leadership skills that were a welcome asset to any unit, but he consistently let his headstrong nature alienate himself from too many of the people who served with him.

The Falcon was the guy who I argued with the most during my yearlong tour. We disagreed on pretty much everything except killing Taliban. Part of this had to do with our diametrically opposed positions on the political spectrum. Part of it had to do with our completely opposing religious views (I am an atheist and he thinks he sits in the right hand of the Lord). But the most personal and aggravating part of our personal dysfunctional relationship had to do with an anomaly that existed in our small unit, an anomaly that frankly alienated not just myself from the Falcon, but also alienated most if not all the officers who comprised half of our sixteen-man team from the Falcon. This anomaly was as simple as it was stark: The Falcon, an NCO, was telling us officers what to do, and getting away with it.

Let me say that again: The Falcon, an NCO, gave qualified, competent, and battle-hardened commissioned officers orders. He had de facto command on missions, and had far more influence on day-to-day affairs with our commander than the commander's own staff did. Through some twist of fate, the Falcon was put into a *Freaky Friday* universe of rank reversal that pissed us officers off beyond belief.

Even before we arrived at our mobilization station, the Falcon had cemented his role as our commander's Rasputin. Credit either the Falcon's wisdom, cunning, and strong will, or our team commander's lack of these traits, but the fact remained that an NCO was running the show.

This aberration was the cause of many humiliating hours of huddled griping and cursing by the officers of the unit, all aimed at the Falcon and our commander for allowing this distortion to occur. I'd like to take a moment to stress the point to those who are not in the military, and who may cheer at the idea of the underdog taking charge and flipping the bird to the officer corps, that the situation was much more complex than our frustration with the reversal of authority. Our unit was a specialized small group of experienced soldiers, and given the nature of our mission (embedded into the Afghan Security Forces), rank really didn't have much importance in day-to-day affairs. It was common to hear NCO's address officers by "dude" instead of "sir," and most of the trappings of military formality between the officer and NCO corps were not in effect. No one had a problem with this. Our lives were already stressful enough dealing with Afghans calling us infidels, so we didn't sweat customs and courtesies too much.

So to have an experienced and wise NCO like the Falcon involved in planning, reviewing, and running missions was normal. There were very few of us, and we needed—to use a Navy phrase—all hands on deck. But the unbridled authority he was given, multiplied by the arrogance than came with it, made for a toxic mix that was too much for most of my officer brethren to handle. We resented that our relationship with the Falcon was essentially turning a couple hundred years of military tradition on its head.

When you compound these conflicts over politics, religion, and the NCO-officer relationship, it should be no surprise that the two of us were always in disagreement and vociferous about it. It became one of my personal pet projects, egged on by fellow officers in the unit, to try to right the wrong and put the Falcon back in his appropriate position on the totem pole. A task made all the more challenging by the fact that I liked him, and consider him to this day to be a friend and comrade in arms.

The Falcon, for all his faults, was an extremely well-traveled and wise soldier. Uncle Sam was lucky to have him in the ranks. But as time passed, a series of events unfolded that allowed me an opportunity to finally confront the Falcon and fix that aberration on the totem pole. It was nearing the end of our cold and gray winter, and a spring cleaning of the FOB was in order. Falcon, who was the highest ranking NCO in our unit, proclaimed one morning at our staff meeting that we needed to destroy a full pallet of meals ready to eat (better known as MREs in Army jargon). I'm guessing there were at least a hundred cases of MREs in the pallet, each case holding about a dozen meals. The meals cost about six to eight dollars each, so we were talking about at least 10,000 dollars in supplies he was proposing to destroy.

Now on the surface, his proclamation that the MREs needed to get tossed didn't raise too many eyebrows. He said they were no longer fit for human consumption. And given that we destroy supplies deemed no longer serviceable all the time in the army, it didn't seem like an outrageous decision.

When he said they were spoiled, I didn't bother asking him how he had come to that conclusion. No one else did, either. He must have had a good reason to make this determination, and I wasn't going to question his plan of action. He knew his stuff, and I accepted that.

But days later, when I overheard two other unit members talking about the planned bonfire of MREs, I was struck by an obvious flaw in logic as to why the MREs were no longer edible. The Falcon had determined that since the MREs had been stored outside and had been exposed to repeated freezing and thawing, they had spoiled and were no longer edible. Back in the day of the brown-bag MREs (old school), when the Falcon had cut his teeth as a young buck soldier, this probably was a correct determination.

But MREs have advanced since the 1980s, and every MRE case today has written in large letters on its side *DO NOT ROUGH HANDLE WHEN FROZEN.* The logical deduction I made from this warning is that MREs *can* be frozen, but should not be handled roughly *when* frozen.

I approached the proposed destruction of the meals like a classic high school– level Scholastic Aptitude Test logic question. If A = B, and B = C, then A= C. My determination was that A+B didn't equal C, and the foodstuffs were still fine to eat. Seeing as this pallet of MREs had spent the winter motionless, there had been no rough handling at all while they were frozen, ergo, they were still edible.

I knew my conclusion was logical and made sense, but it wasn't enough for me to go against the Falcon yet. The Falcon was as stubborn as he was smart, and his normal response to someone questioning his plans was to dig in his heels and go on the offensive against the person who questioned his wisdom. He didn't take criticism very well.

As already stated, our commander relied heavily on the Falcon for guidance. The Falcon was his right-hand man. He was the Cheney to our commander's Bush. Sometimes we wondered who was really running the show, and a lot of times we felt like the Falcon was. This would have been fine if he *was* the commander, but he was an NCO, and it was not in the scope of his duty position nor responsibilities to play this role as long as there were living, breathing officers in the unit.

So I knew if I brought up my concerns in the staff meeting that burning the MREs would be wasting thousands of dollars of government property, I would be gunned down by our commander. I needed more ammo than a logical argument.

After I heard my teammates explain the proposed reason for the Falcon's burn plan, I walked over to my hootch, cracked open my laptop, checked the countdown program to see how many thousands of seconds had passed since the last update, and set about on a search for undisputable proof that would save the MREs from their planned destruction.

I Googled the manufacturer of MREs, and sure enough, they had an information page about their product, which included an in-depth explanation about freezing, thawing, and rough handling. Turns out that rough handling while frozen can cause micro-rips in the plastic lining of the bags containing the preserved food, allowing bacteria to enter and grow when they thawed out. But the manufacturer stated that it could take literally hundreds of freezes and thaws, coupled with rough handing, before these micro-rips would occur. I had found the info I needed, from the manufacturer no less, to save the MREs and the American taxpayers.

The next morning at the regular staff meeting, I brought up the issue, thinking it was going to be a slam dunk. I went at it fully applying the law of Occam's razor, narrowing down my argument to a simple logical and provable thesis on why the MREs were still good. But instead it was I who got cut. Falcon wasn't interested in my facts or logic, and the commander wasn't interested in bucking his right-hand man.

I was shocked. To add injury to insult, the normally politically conservative bunch of soldiers present, who railed against government waste and spending during our regular evening political debates and discussions, all of a sudden had no problem with torching 10,000 dollars' worth of perfectly good government supplies for no good reason except that Falcon said to do it.

I let the issue go, knowing that it wasn't the time and place to win this argument. I knew I would only be asking for trouble by jumping the chain of command and pushing my appeal to higher levels in the hope of divine intervention. But about a week after I was shot down, I overheard one of my buddies mention that he had just seen some Afghans loading up the MREs to bring them to the trash dump outside our FOB. I felt an urge to make one last-minute appeal to our commander to stop the wasteful burn plan. I slipped into my Crusader mode and decided to make one final stand.

I went into my commander's office, and fortunately he was alone. Without the Falcon by his side, he was a different man. He was more inclined to listen to our suggestions, and showed more freedom in making independent decisions. I made my case, citing the manufacturer's own specifications on the issue of freezing and thawing. He heard me out, and even agreed with my argument, but with a smile on his face, said it was out of his hands. He said his boss, the FOB commander, had authorized the burn, and if I wanted to waste my time and try to convince him of my argument, I should go talk to him. I had his permission to do so. He leaned back in his chair, thinking the issue was finally put in the "done" column. He bid me adieu, and got back to his Internet chat with a woman he was courting on MySpace.

I walked out of his office and made a beeline for the FOB commander. At this point of the story, I need to get off my high horse, pontification about waste, abuse, and fraud prevention, and reveal that part of my drive to stop this MRE burn was something more akin to a personal crusade to be the first guy on the FOB to finally put a chink in the Falcon's armor of invincibility and all-knowing prowess. It's not that I disliked the Falcon; on the contrary, he was a funny guy, very smart in matters tactical and computer related (he single-handedly kept us up and running with wireless Internet access, and was the go-to guy if we got a stubborn computer virus on our laptops). All in all, the Falcon was a super-stud soldier and a great guy's guy. But for too long, I, and for most of our unit, had been privately frustrated with always running into a brick wall when we had an idea about how to do something that was better than what the Falcon had proposed. And this was especially true for us officers, who had grown tired of taking orders from an NCO, no matter how smart or experienced he was.

It wasn't supposed to be this way in the military: An NCO running missions while officers sat back like privates, being told what to do and how to do it. We ached at the chance to bring balance to our little military universe. We were always looking for a chance to publicly and openly put the Falcon back down where he belonged on the chain of command. I had come close once, when I had correctly refused an order from the Falcon and the commander to put snow chains on my Humvee, after I had gathered intel from truck drivers that the roads were snow-free where we were headed. I had informed the Falcon and the commander of this intel, but in their stubbornness, they refused to change the order. In a huff of protest, I just flat-out refused to comply with their order and kept the chains off my Humvee. After a couple miles of travel on snowless roads, the snow chains on all the other vehicles had broken, which had done additional damage to the wheel wells of the vehicles as the irons whipped around and flailed into the under body of the Humvees.

The rhythmic thuds of loose chains shredding into the wheel well and the loud clanking got the commander and the Falcon to realize they made a mistake by ordering the use of chains. They called on the radio to stop the convoy. Everyone was ordered to pull off the remaining chains that hadn't already broken off.

I took the opportunity to walk down to the Falcon's truck and very loudly and publicly call him out for not listening to my advice. The Falcon and I had a toe-to-toe shouting match, which involved a hefty amount of expletives. We later joked about it, recalling the shocked look on the faces of young privates and specialists who watched in amazement as a captain and a first sergeant were screaming at each other and about to start throwing punches. I think the only thing that kept us from actually rolling around on the ground in a violent fit was the fact we were surrounded by Afghans who potentially wanted to kill us. So we stepped back from our pissing contest and loaded back up into the vehicles. Seeing as the commander never once came back to me and acknowledged I had been correct about the snow tires, nor changed his Rasputin-like relationship with the Falcon, I felt the snow-tire fight had not accomplished the larger goal of re-establishing the correct balance between officers and the Falcon. So when the MRE issue popped up, I felt this was a good battlefield to fight it out on.

So, with this personal mini-vendetta fueling my outrage over the waste of thousands of dollars of perfectly good food, I quickly found the higher HQ commander, apologized for the interruption, and talked him through the rapidly developing MRE bonfire. Little did I know it was all for naught, as gasoline was at that very moment being poured on the cardboard cases of MREs as I carefully explained the debacle that I hoped to prevent. By the time I was finished, the commander told me the only reason he had agreed to allow the hundreds of meals to be destroyed was that my commander had told him it was necessary. He said if the facts were as I had presented them, then the MREs should not be burned. I left his office and headed back to my commander's office. As I walked there, I could see a black plume of smoke rising just outside our FOB walls, and I knew I was too late. The MREs were ablaze.

Attempting to salvage at least a pyrrhic victory in the situation, I walked back to my commander's office, and told him that the HQ commander had agreed I was right and they shouldn't be burned. It was clear my boss wasn't happy that I had gone and spoken to the HQ commander, even though he had given me permission to do so. He never expected me to have the balls to go do it, and I could tell he was pissed I had made him look bad by exposing the flawed logic of the Falcon, which he had embraced. I had won the battle but lost the war.

This spray-painted logo that fittingly greeted anyone who entered the Falcon's hootch.

11

THE PREACHER

A quick head count of my small, sixteen-man unit shows that about half of us who were married when we deployed to Afghanistan are now divorced. Everyone has heard the sobering statistics on divorce among soldiers in the Army today, and the frequent re-deployments don't help in keeping a marriage fully grounded. I am part of this demographic, just another GI Joe who was married when I left for war and fully disengaged by the time I got home. Deciding to pull the trigger on my marriage wasn't easy, and I ping-ponged back and forth until I finally decided to end it. I was never alone in making this decision, as I had guys lecturing me to try and make it work, as well as those urging me to divorce the woman I had been married to for fifteen years. One of the voices I remember the most was the Preacher, a unit member who carefully and respectfully played the role of marriage counselor during our year at war.

Preacher was a great guy. He was a higher ranking field grade officer, as well a senior to me in age and life experience. But he always approached me like a close and equal friend. If you saw him in these moments, you would be reminded of the stereotypical neighborhood priest portrayed in so many movies and TV shows. A five o'clock shadow was ever present on his face, even after he was freshly shaved. He had a large physical build that harkened back to his days of playing college football, and a strong, boisterous voice to accompany it. But during the moments when he was sitting next to you and offering some sage wisdom, he spoke in soft, calming tones that increased the impact of his measured words.

I never felt like he was lecturing me in these times, so don't let the nickname of Preacher fool you. Any negative associations with the term *preacher* (i.e.: know-it-all, overbearing, judgmental, etc.) don't apply; this guy had nothing but positive words and wisdom to offer his troops in trouble.

Preacher was an old-school Catholic. To hear him talk of politics and family values sometimes felt like an anachronism, a throwback to the 1950s. But despite his self-imposed, rigid code of conduct in his personal life, he wasn't one to judge others. He was a harsh critic of the infidelity and of the online Internet-relationship orgy that was going on around him, but he would only voice his complaints about it in private conversation among trusted friends. He never got up on a soapbox to extol his values, and I think he kept a behind-the-scenes advisor role because he didn't wish to alienate his fellow soldiers who held different views.

His faith in marriage was, as far as I can tell, rooted in his religious faith, as well as the love he had for his wife and children. He was sincere when he said he would pray for guys like me who were going through a possible divorce. I am an open and aggressive atheist, but instead of feeling prickly about the whole concept of him praying for me, it felt comforting to know he was wishing me well.

To him, the "d-word" (divorce) was not even an option for his personal life. It was a cop-out. It was an affront to the way things should be. Commitment needed to mean something in this world, and he didn't see any reason why his solid relationship with his wife was special: Everyone should be as committed, with no excuses. Harmony would eventually return to any dysfunctional relationship, it was the natural state of things if both sides just stuck together and worked things out. It was so obvious to him: patience, faith, and hope. The Preacher had it all figured out.

But in affairs of the heart, nothing is as simple as it seems, even for those who hold such strong views. Upon his return home from war, the Preacher found out the hard way it was not only soldiers that change when they get deployed. The family left behind also changes, and his wife had made some decisions that betrayed the Preacher's faith in his marriage.

Today the Preacher lives separated from his wife and kids, pending a final divorce. Ironically, our roles have been reversed, and now I play the well-meaning counselor to him on how to navigate the new, awkward world of dating, of loneliness, and missing the regular contact with our kids. It's awkward for me to be in this position, as I look up to him as a superior is so many ways. I never thought our roles might be switched. I check in with him from time to time, and take the opportunity to offer advice on how to manage this difficult "new normal" life he is going through.

12

DEG

Deg got killed over there.

It's really hard to write about him and capture in words what he meant to us. Even three years now after his death, I cry when I e-mail his sister. Even casually talking to war buddies about Deg is difficult. I can never find the words to do him justice, and it's painful to try to verbalize the emotions. It's like I'm chewing on glass as I struggle to speak about the pain I feel now that he is gone.

So I'll keep it simple and short: Deg was a great soldier. He was the archetypal infantryman: Barrel-chested, salty in both word and deed, and the ever-present cigarette that would appear out of nowhere whenever we found ourselves leaning up against the hood of a Humvee. He knew the risks of being there in Afghanistan, but it never slowed him down. When everyone else was panicked in combat and waiting for the senior-ranking officer to figure out a plan, Deg filled the void and figured out a plan. In these moments, rank meant nothing to Deg, and I thank him for being that way, because more often than not, I was that senior-ranking officer rattled by the gunfire with no clue as to what I should do.

I frequently think about Deg and at night my mind doesn't stop. It wanders somewhere between nightmares about losing him and halcyon dreams that fill me with happiness to see him again. He made such an impression on me that I can vividly remember conversations I had with him, down to the exact words he said with his distinctive Kansas country drawl.

I remember the way he furrowed his brow when I made a decisive move on the chessboard, sweeping away any hope he had of victory. "You fucker!" he would mutter, pausing dramatically to add "sir" at the end of his friendly insult. I can still see the way his hand twitched and shook as he grasped the cheap Afghan cigarettes that he bought by the carton for a couple dollars at the local markets. If his hands shook from frazzled nerves or the stress of war, he never showed it in any other way. With a new cigarette tucked in the corner of his mouth, his gravelly voice would demand "one more game!"

Deg is the face of the blood and treasure we are spending in Afghanistan.

I really hope it's worth the sacrifice.

13

LANCELOT

Perhaps the most stoic, honorable, and unflappable guy I served with was Lancelot. He was a modern-day do-gooder with a pistol on his hip, a rifle on his shoulder, and a smile on his slender knight-like and handsomely sculpted face. I never saw him lose his cool or his focus. When many of us were in conniptions about the daily screwups in war, Lancelot was always taking it in stride.

A great example of this was when Lancelot e-mailed me a video clip taken by one of his soldiers. It highlighted the absurdity of the soldier's experience in combat, where luck sometimes played a far greater role than years of training. The video was taken right after an attack by a group of Taliban on his FOB. The enemy had withdrawn, and Lancelot was leading a group of soldiers out on a patrol to look for anything left behind by the retreating enemy. They discovered an unexploded mortar round that had landed near one of their friendly positions, but had failed to detonate. Lancelot put together a small team of soldiers and they secured the area and devised a plan to dispose of the mortar round.

Lancelot decided he would volunteer to get close to the round and toss a grenade onto it to blow it in place. There was a large rock near the mortar round, which he planned to duck behind for protection after he tossed the grenade. This wasn't a wise thing to do, but given the options, it was pretty much the only thing he could do.

Sensing the drama that was about to unfold, one of Lancelot's unit members pulled out his digital camera and set it on movie mode. The video shows Lancelot slowly creeping toward the round. He pauses, takes out his grenade, tosses it, and ducks behind the large rock for protection. Tense seconds passed, then the grenade explodes, but the results were as unintended as they were comical. The grenade blew the mortar round up into the air, and the video clearly shows the mortar as it flies through the air, spinning like a football, until it lands directly next to Lancelot's interpreter, who was hidden behind another rock at, up to that point in time, a seemingly safe distance. The mortar round clanked to the ground at this poor interpreter's feet, and he instantly jumps into the air, screaming fear-laced obscenities at Lancelot for this unintended outcome.

Throughout the video, Lancelot remained calm, with a smile on his face, un-fazed by the fact he had almost blown his interpreter to smithereens.

These unplanned and undesirable outcomes were par for the course in Afghanistan.

Afghan soldiers he was assigned to train were late for missions: no problem.

They were losing gear, or selling it on the black market: no problem.

His soldiers were too busy getting high, or getting caught in three-way homosexual activities (known among us American soldiers as an "Afghan triple stack") when they should have been pulling guard duty: no problem.

Supplies weren't delivered to his remote FOB: no problem.

He was stranded for days and days at Bagram, living out of a small backpack like a vagabond, waiting for a flight back downrange: no problem.

You get the point. But his calm and unflappable nature wasn't a result of indifference. It wasn't that he didn't care. To the contrary, Lancelot *did* care. And it wasn't that he let these indiscretions go unpunished. He regularly chewed his soldiers' asses like bubble gum. It was that Lancelot never lost his cool. Going apeshit, like too many of the rest of us did, really caused more problems than it solved.

When his battle buddy was killed in action, the worst I can say is that he seemed genuinely sad about it for a socially acceptable amount of time. In contrast, when I lost a battle buddy, it put me in a bad place. I trembled, I cowered, I couldn't sleep, I got meds, and I eventually ended up a sleep-deprived train wreck hallucinating absurd scenarios while out on patrol. But Lancelot seemed genuinely unaffected by the loss of his partner in any measurable way. The guy was emotional Teflon. Nothing bad stuck to him.

Lancelot won good-guy points in other ways too. He was uninterested in the Internet hunt for long-distance ladies. He was young and just before he deployed he had gotten married to an equally attractive young professional lady. He was not involved in the tactical-gear arms race either. He seemed happy with what Uncle Sam issued him for the most part. All in all, Lancelot seemed fully satisfied with his life back home, his job at war, and everything in between.

The year at war eventually passed, and when our tour was coming to an end, most of the guys in my unit had gotten short-timer's disease. We hunkered down in our hootches, avoided unnecessary missions, and spent more time packing, tanning, and reminiscing that we did fighting bad guys. Since some members of our unit had been scattered across eastern Afghanistan, the final month was a time of reconsolidation. About two weeks before the end of our tour, the entire unit had reassembled at our FOB in Paktika, except for Lancelot. He had decided not to take any early transportation back to our rally point, so that he could get in as many missions as possible before leaving Afghanistan.

This seemed absolutely insane to the rest of us, given the fact we were so short on the time left on our countdown clocks, and given that he was stationed at one of the toughest FOBs in the country--right on the Pakistani border, and named after the professional football player Pat Tillman, who had been killed nearby. (I should mention here that Lancelot is also featured in Jon Krakauer's book *Where Men Win Glory*).

FOB Tillman was a place I had visited once. Ground access in and out was a suicidal path of cliffs and improvised explosive devices known as the Manacandow Pass. I can honestly say that during my visit to Lancelot's FOB, I felt the most scared than I had felt visiting any other place in Afghanistan.

And yet there he was, with the end in sight, and the unit waiting for him, still out doing patrols and chasing bad guys on the Af-Pak border.

My commander became frustrated with Lancelot's absence and asked me to e-mail him, as I had been in regular contact with him during the tour via e-mail. I wrote and asked where he was and why he hadn't returned yet to our FOB in Paktika. His response was one you might expect to get from a teenage kid hanging out at the beach looking at girls: Perplexed at why I would want him to leave his wonderful spot and scenery. He wrote that he was out patrolling with his "Joes" (his nickname for the Afghan soldiers he was mentoring), and that he would come to us soon. It was clear that the whole idea of senioritis, or short-timer syndrome, was foreign to him.

But it turns out Lancelot wasn't totally immune to the stresses of war. He got home and unceremoniously divorced his young, professional, and equally attractive wife. He also realized that he hated the career he had just begun before deploying (teaching), and quit his job. And finally, he decided to volunteer for another year in the sand. He still e-mails me on occasion from his contractor job in the Middle East. And it still seems like no matter how crappy or boring his job is, he still is having a good time working with his Joes.

14

REBEL

H ad you walked into Rebel's living quarters on our FOB in Paktika, you would have found a pretty average-looking hootch. Plywood and cement brick walls, no windows, and a musty odor formed the backdrop to his array of tactical gear strewn all over his bed. Some items hung on nails on the wooden walls and others were piled up in a haphazard mound in the corner.

The modern United States Army is great at equipping us in every conceivable way for every possible contingency, but it has failed miserably in providing us with enough space in which to store it all. Our living quarters in Afghanistan were small and only semi-private, with a poncho liner hung over the open entrance providing the semblance of a door.

Rebel's hootch, like most others, was littered with the tools and vices of war. Weapons, cleaning rags, and gun lubricant fought for shelf space with spit cups. For those not familiar with the concept of the spit cup, affectionately referred to as the "spitter" by some, it's a field-expedient spittoon used by soldiers who dip or chew tobacco.

Spit cups can range from highly personalized works of art covered in green army tape and hand-drawn designs, to a one-and-done disposable undecorated empty water bottle. A few hard-core soldiers swallow tobacco juice, but for the majority of us, spitting it out was the proper course of action. Given the never-ending supply of bottled water we had around, spit cups and bottles were a regular sight on tables, floors, Humvee dashboards, and lining the shelves in our hootches.

Rebel was a professional-grade tobacco chewer. He had long cut, fine cut, and leaf tobacco. Red Man chew was his favorite. He, like Mr. OCD, had an impressive cache of smokeless tobacco products scattered around his hootch.

Halfway through our tour, and despite Rebel's friendly offers for free dip, I quit dipping tobacco. No longer would tobacco juice stains cover my notebooks and gear. I had hit bottom, chain-dipping Skoal to the point that my gums hurt and my inner lip had shriveled up and looked like a pink prune, much like your fingertips look after you've spent an hour in a hot bathtub.

I loved dip. I still do. But I had crossed a line and needed to get control over my addiction.

During the hot summer months, when combat seemed endless and the string of wounded and dead among Americans and ANA soldiers was long and unbroken, I longed for the cold of winter and the peace it would bring. But war in the winter here becomes numbingly tedious. Cabin fever sets in. Now that it was winter, and I was feeling more and more claustrophobic in our tiny hootches, I began to wish for the summer to return. Dipping became the way to pass the long and uneventful days. We would sit around the common room in our hootch, or in the TOC, and just smoke and dip and spit and smoke and dip and spit. We measured the passage of time by the filling of spit bottles. Had you showed me a bottle during these winter days, I could have told you what time of day it was given by the level of brown, syrupy fluid contained inside it. An inch was morning. Two inches deep was lunchtime. Anything above that was late afternoon. In the evening, the bottle would be tossed, retired unceremoniously, and a new bottle would be brought into the rotation for the following day.

While we are on the subject of bodily-fluid containers adorning our hootches, let me introduce you to a close cousin of the spitter. It was a needed and dear friend to all soldiers during cold winter nights: the piss bottle.

When it's too cold at night to get up, don a winter layer of clothing, strap on a pistol, and walk fifty meters to the latrine, we resort to the piss bottle. It only takes a couple of tries to master the technique of pissing in an empty water bottle in the dark without spillage, so it quickly became a regular bedside item. Even Mr. OCD would resort to using this soldier variation of the bedpan, and would risk violating the sanctity of his sleeping area with a little spilled tinkle in order to avoid the dark, wintry trek and stay warm on a cold Afghan night.

The real problem with piss bottles wasn't the risk of spraying urine all over the place in the dark. It was that in the pitch black of the night, piss bottles look and feel just like regular water bottles. Absent a disciplined system of bottle organization by your bed, it was easy to grab the wrong bottle for the task at hand in the darkness of night.

Many a time I grabbed a bottle, thinking it was a mostly empty piss bottle, only to quickly have urine overflow onto the floor because what I had in fact grabbed was an almost full water bottle. Picture the frantic search for an empty bottle, in the black of night, while warm liquid is dripping through the fingers of the hand holding the overflowing bottle. Not a proud moment in any man's life.

Then there is the opposite problem: Mistaking the piss bottle for a thirst-quenching clean water bottle. I'm man enough to admit that on a couple occasions, in a half sleep, I'd woken up from my never-ending fight with dehydration and accidentally taken a swig from what I thought was a water bottle, only to projectile vomit out the cold urine once it hit my taste buds.

I may be alone in admitting this mix-up, but I know I wasn't alone in experiencing it. On a couple occasions I was awoken by the late-night unmistakable retching coming from a neighbor's hootch who had made the same mistake of taking a swig off a spitter or piss bottle in the darkness.

In addition to causing these disgusting late-night moments, piss bottles also provided a form of entertainment and scientific discovery for us. We'd let them sit for days to watch the urine separate into different layers and color variations. Rebel didn't keep his around long enough to witness this metamorphosis of urine. Instead, he made it a daily ritual to pour his bottles out on a tire chain that was sitting on the ground outside our hootch. He monitored the corrosion from the urine on the iron chain over the weeks, comparing it against the "control group" of tire chains, unexposed to urine, which sat a couple of feet away.

For the rest of us, piss bottles were eventually collected up and thrown unceremoniously into the large garbage cans outside our hootches. The garbage cans would then be picked up daily by Afghan locals who worked on our FOB, and brought to the dump right outside the FOB walls. At the dump, the garbage would be professionally looted by an army of Afghan children, who never let anything go to waste. I wonder how many of them also took a swig off of the mystery lemonade bottles before they caught on as to what it really was.

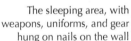

A pretty typical view of the hootch, with some spit cups and water bottles in the lower left corner.

The sleeping area, with weapons, uniforms, and gear hung on nails on the wall

15

RAINBOW

I want to be clear at the outset of this: I am 100 percent in support of gay and lesbian soldiers openly serving in the United States Armed Forces. My experiences have shown me that they are just as qualified, motivated, and patriotic as their hetero comrades-in-arms.

The reasons for keeping homosexuals out are lame prejudices from a bygone era when people feared some predatory homosexual stereotype that would assault you in the showers or try to kiss you in a foxhole. These stereotypes just don't pan out in the reality of military life.

Fortunately, these prejudices are dying a slow but steady death, and I am confident that my children, should they choose to serve in the military, will serve with openly gay and lesbian soldiers. And at the rate things are going in Afghanistan, my children will likely also have an opportunity to serve in that fun little corner of the world.

I have no problem being open about how I feel about homosexual soldiers, but unfortunately I can't be as forward about identifying who these soldiers may be. Given that, at the time of this writing, "don't ask, don't tell" is still in effect, and given that gay and lesbian soldiers walk a tightrope between their sexuality and their military careers, I don't want to be the guy who inadvertently outs a man who clearly doesn't want to be outed.

With that in mind, I'll share with you a bare minimum of detail about the soldier I call Rainbow, who honorably volunteered and served in support of his country's efforts in Afghanistan.

Rainbow never came out to any of us during the time we served together in Afghanistan. Under current regulations he couldn't. But I got strong pings on my "gaydar" the first time I met him. Suffice to say, they were classic signs there for anyone who was paying attention.

For a couple months, we lived on the same FOB. All the guys in our barracks would regularly be on our cell phones, laying in bed, calling back to the States and talking to our wives and girlfriends throughout the night.

But not Rainbow.

The only calls we ever heard him make in his hootch were to his family. Our barracks were not noise-proof, so any phone calls were basically broadcast to anyone present in their hootches.

Rainbow never made the kind of the sappy romantic calls to a loved one that we were always engaged in. Instead, late at night, after everyone was well asleep, Rainbow would get up and go outside the hootch and climb up into one of the unmanned fighting positions. There, he would spend hours in whispered conversation with someone special. I usually pounded lots of bottles of water before I went to bed, and sure enough every night, if I didn't have a piss bottle handy, I'd be getting up out of bed at about 2:00 AM to take a leak at the latrines.

Since it was the dog days of summer, I could comfortably walk to the latrine in shorts and a T-shirt. I'd grab my pistol, leave my hootch, and walk out into the silent and magnificent Afghan night. I would be greeted by a sea of beautiful stars that littered the nighttime sky and would stand there for a couple of magical seconds, and let my eyes adjust to the darkness. Then I would scan the FOB's walls for Taliban silhouettes, and once I was sure it was clear of any boogeymen, I'd confidently stroll over to the latrine. This short walk would take me within earshot of where Rainbow sat, in the shadow of the fighting position, whispering words to someone far away.

I never tried to eavesdrop on him or his conversations, but there were times when his tone of voice betrayed the fact he was engaged in a romantic conversation with a significant other. Giggles, sweet nothings, and long good-byes are pretty easy to detect, even in passing.

I didn't care if he was talking to his gay lover. I knew Rainbow was a squared-away professional soldier. He clearly wanted privacy, and he deserved it. Unfortunately, a lot of guys in the unit didn't feel the same way. My hunches about his homosexuality, as I said already, were shared among many in the unit. But this was not a welcome fact for many of my comrades. Some guys felt threatened by something different that they didn't understand or didn't agree with. A bunch of the guys from the South were the most vocal in their homophobia, but in fairness there were also a couple of redneck northerners who weren't too friendly toward "the fags and queers" either.

I remember one officer from Texas laying into Rainbow pretty hard for spending too much time hanging out with the Afghan interpreters. It was common knowledge that while the Afghans publicly deplored homosexuality as a sin, given the absence of women in their lives, Afghan males did a lot of hand-holding, snuggling, and sleeping together. So to this Texas officer, it made sense that Rainbow would be lovey-dovey with the interpreters all the time, as his sexual preference fit right into the Afghan way of doing things.

Rainbow wasn't the first homosexual soldier I had served with. Over the course of my military career, I had the honor of serving with a handful of homosexual soldiers. Frankly, in every case, they tended to be better soldiers than their heterosexual peers. Maybe it was because they had more to prove. Not one of them was publicly "out" (they couldn't be, or they would have been separated from the military), but the clues and hints were out there for the perceptive. A triangle or rainbow bumper sticker on a car parked in the armory parking lot was one clue I'd seen many times. Another was a constant reference to their "partner," who never seemed to be available for any military social functions or unit events. These were perhaps hints offered to the people they may have wanted to know, while retaining just enough plausible deniability to preserve their military career.

Interestingly, not all homosexual soldiers were discriminated on equally by the homophobes in uniform. The male gay soldiers, for various reasons, were less accepted than the lesbian ones. After all, lesbian porn is a staple of infantry life, so it was pretty hard for even a devout homophobe to hate on lesbians. As a bumper sticker I saw in a soldier's hootch in Afghanistan best put it, *I SUPPORT GAY RIGHTS, AS LONG AS IT'S TWO HOT LESBIANS.*

In Afghanistan, it was a running joke that our higher brigade's logistical task force (LTF.) had so many women in it that it was referred to as the "lesbian task force." This nickname was rooted in some truth. Quite a few of the females in the LTF acted and presented themselves more like men than women. These ladies, in civilian parlance, were the "bull dykes" of the Army. They wore crew cuts, no makeup, and were more likely to be seen with a cigarette dangling from their lips and some dirt on their cheeks.

Given all this as a backdrop, its easy to see how homophobic colleagues and policies like "don't ask, don't tell" kept good guys like Rainbow hiding in the closet. If Rainbow was gay, he couldn't tell anyone or he would be run out of the military. And if he wasn't, the prejudicial attitudes were there anyway to the detriment of other soldiers who were.

I never asked Rainbow what was up with his love life. I just hope my actions and comments around him let him know that if he, or any other homosexual soldiers for that matter, "played for the other team," I was cool with that.

This is the area behind our barracks where Rainbow would sit at night and have his private phone conversations.

16.

JACK

L et me tell you about Jack. Jack was every man in Afghanistan. He was a normal guy with normal needs.
He was issued lots of gear to help him survive his tour in
Afghanistan, but one critical piece of equipment was sorely
lacking. That essential item, which had been something Jack
had grown accustomed to his whole life back in the good old
U.S.A., was women.

Over in Afghanistan, women were pretty much removed from our daily lives. It wasn't like Nam, where hook-
ers roamed the streets, and platoons of little mama-san girlfriends were out there trying to land a GI for the night. It
wasn't even close.

Afghan women were forbidden to us. If you were lucky
enough to even see one, chances are she was covered head
to toe in a burkha. I only saw an occasional Afghan woman
uncovered in public in the capital city of Kabul, which was a
much less conservative environment. And you would see an
occasional Afghan woman out in the wastelands, among a
remote and isolated group of nomads called the Kuchis.

Kuchi women are an interesting lot. They come from
a tribe that does not subscribe to the Muslim rule of covering of women head to toe. On the contrary, they wore the
most eclectic, colorful, and flamboyant attire I ever saw in
Afghanistan, and there is no burkha involved. Kuchi women
stand out like a shining beacon of femininity in a wasteland
of men and goats.

The problem with Kuchi women, at least from my war-
stressed, female-starved, and admittedly judgmental and
objectifying war-time perspective, was that because Kuchi
women live perhaps one of the hardest lives on the planet,
fully exposed to the destructive rays of the Afghan sun, de-
livering children in large quantities, and existing on a diet of
dust and hard labor, they age at a rate that makes it difficult

to enjoy the view, so to speak. Frankly, most of the Kuchi women we saw up close looked like leather-faced mummies. Their skin resembled the look and texture of a baseball glove, with a matrix of wrinkles running across it like dried creek beds. A woman who looked eighty could have easily been forty, and a girl of the age of fifteen could pass for twenty-five. The nomadic lifestyle in Afghanistan was not kind to the individual beauty needs and hygiene standards of Kuchi women.

Having said these harsh but honest truths about the ungraceful aging of Kuchi women, if you got a peek at a young Kuchi girl in her mid- to late teens, before she had been transformed by the sun and the harsh desert lifestyle into a leather bag of skin, you would likely be convinced your female-deprived eyes had died and gone to heaven.

Rumor was that Kuchis were very much willing to sell off their daughters for any purpose, whether it was to be a housekeeper, sex slave, sheepherder, or wife. As long as the price was right a deal could be made. If you had the money, and the patriarch had a surplus daughter, wife or aunt, some Kuchi women were for sale, much like the sheep they herded. The going rate at the time I was there was rumored to be 5,000 dollars. It was a price few could pay, but there are Afghans who, despite the poverty around them, have incredible amounts of money. Afghanistan has many billionaires (drug warlords), who in turn have even more sub-warlord millionaires on their payrolls. The drug money flows down throughout the organization to all its managers, so I'm sure there are plenty of young men who would have the 5,000 dollars handy if they saw a Kuchi woman they liked who was for sale.

Personally, I know of no American who bought a Kuchi girl. It runs against our basic national moral consensus on slavery and the sex trade. However, I'd be a liar if I didn't admit to playing the devil's advocate about the merits of making such a purchase. It was the kind of philosophical debate we indulged in to pass boring nights in the hootch. We cooked up hypothetical scenarios of all kinds. Would you rather lose a foot in combat or both thumbs? Would you rather be

surrounded by Taliban or be stuck in the middle of a mine-
field? The list of moral dilemmas and ethical conundrums
was unending. So when the conversation came one night to
the issue of purchasing a Kuchi woman, I made a pretty good
moral argument for making such a deal.

Here is how it could work, and how it would be justifi-
able given our generally agreed-upon understanding of human rights. First off, financing wouldn't be a problem. FOO
rules were bent every day, paying for all sorts of services and
contracts that were technically not permitted under the program. People bought cable TV and called it electrical wiring
repairs. Others bought sheep for food and said the money
was spent on urgent target-practice operations.

As for the issue of human rights and women's rights, I
never argued in favor of keeping a woman in a permanent
state of sex slavery or domestic servitude. My goal was short
term. It was clearly self-serving to our FOB, but by the reasoning of my argument, it would also be beneficial to the
Kuchi woman. I built a framework that envisioned a truly
symbiotic relationship.

I based my justification for this purchase on the premise
that modern female slavery is a given fact of life in Afghanistan. Kuchi women, like most women in Afghanistan, are
treated like property and at best third-class citizens. In many
cases, it appeared that they got less attention and care than
the livestock they tended, and they lived the hardest life I've
ever seen (and I've been in some pretty tough and desper-
ate parts of the world). Kuchi culture has evolved to be this
way, and thousands of young Kuchi women will continue
to live out their short and difficult lives with no schooling,
dental care, medical care, proper nutrition, or freedom from
grinding poverty. The buying and selling of Kuchi women is
a time-honored tradition, so my proposal to buy one was not
breaking any of their social norms.

On our side of the moral equation, thousands of young
international boys and girls are regularly removed from dismal social situations of neglect and abuse when large cash
payments are made to their host countries' governments

or privately funded organizations. These children are then shipped to America. We don't call this slavery. We call it international adoption. No one claims it to be immoral or unjust. To the contrary, we celebrate the fact that we are giving a child the chance to leave a horrible situation and enjoy life. I personally support this process and the altruistic intentions behind it, and have two adopted children from Ethiopia who I cherish as much as my own biological kids.

So by extension, by purchasing a Kuchi woman, I argued that we would be doing something both morally and economically positive, much like international adoption. On all Afghan FOBs there are Afghans employed as housekeepers. On our FOB, we had two guys who cleaned, did laundry, cut hair, and made runs to town to buy us whatever items we needed. They were paid large amounts of money, which reflected an American pay scale instead of the Afghan pay scale of their country. These FOB "maids" were by Afghan standards millionaires, making more money than doctors and lawyers would ever dream of making in the broken Afghan economy. The 5,000-dollar price tag for a Kuchi woman was but a fraction of our FOB maid's annual salary, so right off the top by buying one for our base we would be saving Uncle Sam thousands of dollars over the course of her employment.

Secondly, our two male maids spent a lot of time learning English from us, learning how to use the Internet, etc. We embraced them like family and made sure that they received all the intellectual, ideological, and business acumen we could offer them in the course of their daily interactions with us. The maids who worked on our FOB left there filthy rich, with some English-speaking skills and lots of savvy on how to operate in the newly transforming and slowly modernizing Afghan society.

So given that we already hire Afghans to do this type of work at extremely overinflated prices, and given that Kuchi women already are traditionally bought and sold, and given the improvements of the quality of life for anyone who came and lived on and worked on our FOB, it seemed like a good idea.

Would it have been illegal to use FOO money to buy what essentially would have been a slave girl? Absolutely. But as I've stated already, the illegality of a FOO purchase rarely stopped anyone from spending money on something they weren't supposed to spend it on. Receipts were fudged and justifications for the purchase were stretched to the point of absurdity on many occasions.

Would it have been an opportunity for some good things to happen to this young Kuchi woman, vis-à vis education, literacy, and an improved living standard? Absolutely.

Would she have been able to grow up in an environment that didn't violently and ruthlessly discriminate against her for being a female? Absolutely. I think we all could agree that Afghanistan needs a lot more liberated female types among its population to get the gender-equality revolution jump-started, and maybe spending one's formative teenage years among Westerners would be a drop in the bucket of accomplishing this goal.

When she left her employment there--either because of the war had ended, or because she expressed a desire to move on—would she be an incredibly wealthy and financially independent woman? Absolutely.

American soldiers are generous when it comes to the Afghan nationals we work with. We passed our maids envelopes stuffed with cash for holidays, baby births, marriages, and a myriad of other special occasions. I'm confident that this hypothetical Kuchi slave would have walked off that FOB a few years down the road with an envelope full of cash that would far exceed what the average Kuchi woman would earn in her entire lifetime.

But we can't forget that we are dealing with young, horny men deprived of any exposure to women. Given this, would it have been a good idea to put a teenage girl in a testosterone-charged environment like this? Would it have been a good idea, given that she would be the only woman these soldiers had seen for months? Would we as soldiers have been able to separate her sexuality from all these positive things aforementioned? Absolutely not.

It's safe to say that there won't be any Kuchi women working on American FOBs in the near future, if ever. It remains just another pipe-dream philosophy debate for bored and horny soldiers spending their downtime missing women and trying to rationalize a way to return them to our daily existence.

So let's get back to the main subject of this story: Jack. The fact that no one is getting a teenage Kuchi maid in the immediate future, and that all other Afghan women are not part of our lives in any way over there, leaves us with only one pool of women who are around and somewhat accessible: the American female soldiers serving alongside us. Female soldiers were pretty much only present on the large logistical FOBs, because women are still forbidden to be placed in combat arms duty positions. And even on large logistical FOBs, there definitely weren't enough single women to meet every guy's wish for a female companion. Some of these women soldiers were happily married or had boyfriends back home. They made it clear they were off limits, although that wasn't always how things played out.

One of the troopers you've read about in this book spent our train-up months in Mississippi courting a married female sergeant, to no avail. But after about four months of hot days in Afghanistan, she eventually obliged his advances. On a visit to her large FOB for a logistical resupply, they had sex in her unit's supply room, with her bent over a rifle rack.

It may be easy for people to read that and condemn such infidelity, but don't do it until you have walked in their combat boots. Until you've gone months with no contact with the opposite sex, and you are literally facing death every day, morality changes and civilian norms no longer hold much weight.

For me personally, I got to the point that I would have given up my long-held belief in marital fidelity simply because I was convinced I was never going to make it home alive. Life is too short in war, and soldiers live for the day at hand, and accept the price of guilt and the fallout from their transgressions that may come if they are lucky enough to make it home alive.

Not all female soldiers had hang-ups about being sexually active in Afghanistan. Many didn't bother playing hard to get. Instead, they assumed the role of a modern-day Florence Nightingale turned sex therapist for horny guys, and slept with as many soldiers as they could. I heard rumors of a voluntary U.S. military whorehouse, so to speak, being run at our brigade's headquarters. According to the rumors circulating down range, a group of female Florida National Guard soldiers held court weekly in a clandestine location on this logistical FOB. It could have been true, or it could have been wishful thinking on the part of horny soldiers. Either way, the legend of the "Florida cathouse" made its way throughout Afghanistan.

Aside from the two female extremes of faithfully married and eager beavers, the rest of the female soldiers in Afghanistan were somewhere in the middle of this sliding scale of sexual activity. It was tough either way for female soldiers, trying to balance a sense of self-respect and self-control. It's fair to say the deck is stacked against female soldiers in this sexually deprived environment. Women have the same needs as men, but they have to deal with the double standard of sexual relations in our culture: A guy who got laid a lot was a stud. A woman who did the same thing was a slut.

So, with this lengthy introduction to the limited sexual landscape as it exists in Afghanistan, let's finally get back to our original subject: Jack. Like I said at the onset, Jack was really every man. Jack had sexual needs, and no matter what his marital status back home was, he was going to go crazy if he didn't have some type of sexual release. This usually came in the form of jacking off in what became euphemistically known as "Jack's shack", or "the Jack shack."

The fact is that there wasn't anyone in my unit named Jack. And when I said that Jack was every man in Afghanistan at the outset of this story, I meant it. Everyone eventually paid a visit to Jack's shack, which was nothing more than a code name for your hootch during those moments of extreme sexual frustration that just had to be released. One's hootch would magically transform into a Jack shack when one was in there taking care of business.

The subject of jacking off is still taboo in polite civil society, but in the military, the performance of all the private bodily functions are celebrated public announcements. Being crude is the name of the game in combat arms units. So if you were going to leave the TOC and go to the bathroom, you would stand up and loudly announce to everyone within earshot: "I'm going to go take a dump." If you were going to leave the motor pool and go rub one out, you'd tell your buddies: "I'm going to the Jack shack, don't bother me for the next ten minutes."

The Jack shack wasn't the only place to relieve the buildup of sexual tension. The other commonly used location was the showers. My all-time favorite slang term I learned in Afghanistan came from this secondary location. I recall the story as told to me by the Falcon, of a first sergeant standing in front of his company formation, lambasting his soldiers for wasting water. At the time, there was an influx of new soldiers in country, and their FOB resources were being stretched to the breaking point. Potable water shortages were a serious short-term problem. So there was this first sergeant, in the heat of midday, stomping around in front of his formation, yelling insults and threats to get his weary soldiers' attention about water preservation.

"And if I catch any one of you making 'shower babies,' I'm gonna see that you get written up!"

Shower babies! Now that was a classic army metaphor, to say the least. It turns out that these soldiers had been living in a large communal tent, which afforded no privacy and therefore no Jack shack. So they had done what they had been trained to do; adapt, improvise, and overcome. They had all been jacking off in the shower, causing a large-scale waste of potable water in the process. A shower, according to the lecture from the first sergeant, was a place to scrub your nuts clean, but not to clean your pipes.

On our FOB, we only really had one chronic water waster. Badger was a firm believer in the production of shower babies. He proudly announced that he had accomplished this mission each morning before our staff meeting. Most of the other guys were more Jack shack types. The Jack shack was just a better venue for the act. It was private and didn't waste any water resources so you couldn't get yelled at by a cranky first sergeant. The Jack shack allowed you to use your laptop, which was filled to the gills with gigs of porn. In the shower, you had to rely on your imagination to get you through, which a lot of guys just couldn't do. We all tried it in the shower, but quickly learned that it was just too demanding because we were always mentally tired from the stress. So by far, the majority of dudes preferred the Jack shack.

Like America, which has a schizophrenic relationship with the subject of sex and masturbation (publically conservative and against it, privately a freak that can't get enough of it), Afghan society also has a sexual double standard. Our interpreters would chide us for "making jerk" as they called it. It was forbidden, and quite a few of them told us the fable of the man who jacked off too much and went blind. It is sad to say that even these smart Afghan interpreters, who were far more educated and worldly than the average Afghan, still believed wholeheartedly that the major cause of blindness in their society was "making jerk."

It should be no surprise that these same Afghans, who lectured us on the immorality of jacking off, were the same guys who discreetly borrowed porno DVDs from American soldiers as often as they could.

Our FOB showers, better known as "Badger's shower-baby delivery room."

17

THE GROUNDSKEEPER

The Groundskeeper was an NCO who was long in the tooth, set in his ways, and lacking in the desire or ability to adapt to the changing world that was unfolding around him. He was knee-deep in a non-traditional specialized unit in an unconventional counterinsurgency war, and he was at a lack for coping skills to deal with it. As a result, he opted for his own self-preservation, and burrowed himself into the safe confines of our FOB like a tick on a dog's belly. Because of this approach to the war, it should be no surprise that he was held in low esteem by most of his comrades-in-arms.

During the six months that I served with him in Ghazni Province, I can count on one hand the number of times I saw the Groundskeeper leave the FOB to go out on a combat mission. He was the senior NCO, and as a result very few people were in a position to push him to change his ways. Those who could do this probably recognized his limitations and allowed him to assume the role of FOB superintendant. Thus, his nickname: the Groundskeeper.

If I seem unusually harsh on this fellow, it's because I, along with most of the men who served with him, feel he is directly and personally responsible for a series of events that led to the death of Deg. So take what I have to say with a grain of sugar, as I have an anger that still stews in me years after this unfortunate series of events played out. But I can assure you that my memories of the Groundskeeper are shared by many, and his story remains an ax in need of grinding.

To his credit, the Groundskeeper was on his second tour of duty in Afghanistan. I can't take that away from him. He volunteered for both his yearlong vacations in the sand. His first tour was at a time when the war was basically non-existent. Back in the first couple years of Operation Enduring Freedom, combat was the exception to the norm. It was a rare event that seemed to always happen on the other side of the country, far from where you were stationed. So the Groundskeeper cut his teeth on this military-vacation–like atmosphere and decided to come back for a second go-around.

But Afghanistan had changed a lot since his first visit and his second tour. Gone were the days of easy living in Kabul on a giant Disneyland FOB. This time around, the Groundskeeper had ended up in an area of Ghazni Province that had, in military parlance, recently slipped from green (friendly), to red (enemy controlled). At the time the Groundskeeper had arrived, Ghazni had more American KIAs than any other province in the country. He knew this was a dangerous place, and I think it shaped how he self-defined his job description from being a combat mentor to one that conveniently kept him on the FOB and out of harm's way.

The Groundskeeper's daily schedule was predictable. Every day he would get up, eat chow, have a couple smokes and a cup of coffee, and then set out on the difficult task of slave-driving Afghan day laborers working on our FOB to build B-huts, dig ditches, and fill the Hesco dirt boxes that we used for barricades. All of this was successfully completed from the shaded comfort of the front seat of his Ford Ranger pickup truck.

If you heard him tell it, he was busy at work improving the FOB, overseeing a wide range of contracts and construction projects. But I think he spent most of his time driving around, smoking cigarettes, and drinking coffee. I'm not alone in this conclusion. It was a generally held belief that he was living the life of a fobbit superintendent, while the rest of us were out on blast-filled patrols in hell.

The Groundskeeper clearly deserves credit for supervising some improvements on the FOB, and I won't begrudge him that due. But on every other FOB, a soldier was performing the same FOB improvement projects, *and* supporting combat operations on a regular basis. Fidel was a logistics officer, but he regularly went out in harm's way. Dexter was a logistics officer, but he regularly went out on combat missions. Mr. OCD was an operations and logistics officer, in charge of planning operations, and he regularly went out on combat missions. And finally, the Falcon, who held the same duty position of senior NCO mentor on my second FOB in Paktika, was a regular out on combat patrols. You get my point.

One day, the Groundskeeper was driving around in his Ford Ranger, and he happened to cross paths with Deg. At the time, there had been a dispute among our unit about what combat patches we were authorized to wear, and although trivial, it had resulted in some heated disagreements over the interpretation of shoulder-sleeve insignia regulations. Without going into too much tedious detail, it's important to point out that on this day in question, Deg was wearing the patch of his home state's National Guard. And the Groundskeeper, in keeping in line with his reputation of being a lapdog for our commander (who had wrongly decreed that we were not authorized to wear our home state patches), stopped Deg and ordered him to remove his Kansas National Guard patch. This verbal confrontation set of the series of events that eventually resulted in the death of Deg.

The Groundskeeper was a "patch Nazi" (a term you will be introduced to later in this book), and he reveled in being the enforcer of all things chickenshit. The Groundskeeper never missed an opportunity to be the commander's eyes and ears when something stupid or trivial was going down. He just never understood that in specialized, small units like ours, we leave the trivial chickenshit stuff at the door when we enter a combat environment. Insignificant and minor infractions by anyone threatened the perceived power and authority of the Groundskeeper, so when Deg basically told him to go to hell, the Groundskeeper lobbied successfully to have Deg transferred to another FOB.

The Groundskeeper never had the balls to tell Deg he was working to ship him off, and Deg didn't find out until the day before he was shipped off that he had been transferred. It was a cowardly sneak attack orchestrated by the Groundskeeper.

Within a month of the transfer, Deg was dead. When we heard the news, our initial anger wasn't directed at the Taliban, who had shot Deg in combat. Instead, our anger was directed toward the Groundskeeper for orchestrating his transfer for petty, personal reasons. After I got the word that Deg had been killed, I walked outside the TOC and saw Badger and Ski sitting outside at one of our picnic tables. Deg had been the true father-figure NCO on our FOB, and especially to these younger guys. Badger and Ski were like his sons. They were wiping away tears as they smoked cigarettes with shaky hands. They were cursing and threatening the Groundskeeper up and down, with no reservations about getting in trouble for it. I didn't intervene. I really wasn't in much of a position to do anything myself, as I was choking back tears. If I opened my mouth at that moment, sobs would have been the only things to come out. I don't think any of us every spoke another word to the Groundskeeper for the rest of our tour.

18

SKINTAG

The funny thing about being a soldier is that you don't need to go to war to be damaged physically and mentally. You don't need to deploy to a faraway land to have your marriage fall apart, and your comfortable world back home shatter into little hopeless pieces. Skintag is a perfect example of this phenomenon. He never made it past our initial mobilization station training in Mississippi, and yet I think he may have ended up worse off than most of us who weathered a year of combat in Afghanistan. And given the degrees of PTSD many of us picked up along the way over there, that's saying a lot.

They say that the road to hell is paved with good intentions, and Skintag was full of good intentions when he volunteered to deploy with our small unit to Afghanistan. But his path didn't take him to Paktika or Ghazni. Instead it detoured and landed him in a horrible place far from Afghanistan.

While his mind was eager to finally get a chance to go to war and earn his combat patch, his body refused to comply with this grand plan. Unbeknownst to all of us in our unit, Skintag had a old knee injury that he did his best to conceal, but with only a couple weeks left before we would be packing our bags and flying across the globe, he casually hopped off a footlocker in our hootch, and his knee gave out under him.

He lay on the ground with his leg practically on backwards, grimacing in pain, but assuring us he would be fine. Those standing close enough to him when he fell said they heard a muffled popping sound, which they knew couldn't be good.

Our first reaction was to do everything we could to carry, push, or drag Skintag to the training finish line and get him on the plane with us. But the pain didn't subside, the swelling grew worse, and within hours Skintag was off to the base's medical facility for evaluation.

We knew the outcome wasn't going to be good, and no one was surprised when Skintag got put into a medical holding unit, and then shipped off to larger medical facility in Georgia for rehabilitation and surgery.

I had known Skintag for a couple years before our time in pre-mobilization training in Mississippi. He had been a fellow company commander in our light infantry battalion. He stood out in our infantry unit as a highly experienced and motivated commander. His first sergeant at the time was the Falcon, and the two of them clicked together and had the most high-speed company in the outfit. He was loud, cocky, and overbearing, so he and the Falcon got along just fine. In public he would rip us a new one, mocking our mistakes, constantly jockeying for the pole position of alpha male among the commanders in our battalion. But privately, he was willing to help a fellow officer out with advice and support. When I first got command of Company C, and he saw I was having a hard time with something, he would pull me aside and offer his two cents, with a sincere hope I'd right my ship. He was loyal to his unit and his fellow officers in this way.

So when we reported for our deployment down south for three months of training, I was glad he was along for the ride. Although I knew that back home, Skintag had just had a baby daughter and seemed happily married, but he seemed equally happy to get a chance to go to war. He had been in the military for well for over a decade, with both enlisted and officer time, and hadn't yet gotten a chance to go into harm's way. Among us infantry guys, it's critical to our careers, and our self-esteem, to get a chance to go to war. So family issues aside, Skintag was definitely more than ready.

His bed was about three bunks down from mine in our large communal hootch, next to the Greek's. His raspy voice (from a hearty smoking habit) was one that boomed above the normal din of noise that filled our barracks. But on that eventful day, when he landed wrong and his knee gave out, his voice was instantly removed from the background noise that filled our lives. His wall locker and footlocker filled with gear remained behind for a week in our hootch. Then without warning it was unceremoniously packed up and sent back to his home state. Just like that, he and his possessions were gone. It was as if he had never been there at all.

Literally a whole year passed before I thought about Skintag again. I hadn't heard anything since the news he was being shipped out to Georgia for treatment. Our tour in Afghanistan was almost over, and without sounding coldhearted or indifferent, I had forgotten all about him. War is such an intense experience, and it surrounds you with dozens of new soldiers, new faces, new names, and a seemingly endless array of life-altering experiences, that I had forgotten a lot about my friends and life back home. I forgot the street names of places I'd lived in for years. I forgot birthdays, and restaurant names, and event-important personal memories. And mixed among this hodgepodge of memory, I forgot all about Skintag.

When I heard Falcon mention his name one day during an out-processing meeting in our TOC, my ears perked up and a spark flew across some dark synapses of my brain. I remember saying to myself "Skintag! Holy shit, I had forgotten all about Skintag!"

I assumed he was back home, having a good time with his wife, child, and enjoying a cold beer for all of us who couldn't. Reality couldn't have been further from the truth. Instead of returning to his normal life, Skintag had gotten caught up in all the nightmares of Army medical hold. The injuries to his knee were severe, and he got put into a purgatory status where he was to remain until doctors could figure out what needed to be done, and arrange for it to be completed. This process took over a year, and when surgeries were finally conducted, Skintag remained trapped in this place for months of rehab. He remained the property of Uncle Sam, stuck on active duty awaiting the slow wheels of army medical bureaucracy to turn in his favor with little to do to fill his days.

Having his brothers-in-arms off in harm's way, all the while remaining in a comfy but hellish medical facility Stateside, Falcon told us that Skintag slipped into a serious depression. It's one thing to go to war and get hurt and end up in rehab for months. That scenario is difficult and depressing enough, but in the back of the wounded soldier's mind he can at least say "Well, I gave it my best. I went to war. I wasn't a coward. I played the combat game and got messed up." And the medals and awards will be there as proof. A Purple Heart. A CIB (combat infantryman's badge). Maybe even a Bronze or Silver Star. These things help take the sting out of being removed from the game and sent to the rear to heal.

But Skintag had none of this. He never even made it out of the starting gate. I think this fact ate at him like a cancer. He was stuck in the rear and was powerless to do anything about it. His knee injuries were so severe that it was likely he would be removed from military service and separated from the ranks permanently. And in stark contrast, his peers were now out doing what he had trained and prepared and dreamed of doing for years.

In our previous infantry battalion, where he and I were both company commanders, Skintag was the lion among kittens. He was the officer with the loudest voice and the longest list of true stories. Now he was in a drab medical facility while his peers were out earning their CIBs and combat patches and Bronze Stars. It must have been absolute torture.

I can partially relate to his scenario, in that I spent about three weeks stuck on Bagram Air Base after having an irregular heartbeat and severe dehydration. I went absolutely stir-crazy waiting for the needed medical supplies to arrive in Bagram for the tests that I required to have before I could be returned to duty.

When these testing supplies finally did arrive, I got the okay to return to my FOB in Ghazni, and I was excited to get out of the smothering safety of Bagram. As twisted as it may sound, I had grown to prefer the high-risk lifestyle of bloody combat missions and unrelenting stress.

So yeah, I think I understand what Skintag was feeling as he rotted away in Georgia, reading e-mail reports on exciting combat engagements and challenging missions that he had envisioned himself leading. Instead, he just led himself from medical appointment to medical appointment.

I don't know too much of the rest of Skintag's story beyond the update I got from the Falcon during that staff meeting, but it appears his marriage had pretty much fallen apart. The depression was at a severe and dangerous level, and the Falcon was genuinely worried about what was going to happen to his old buddy.

I never heard again from Skintag, and I haven't asked any of my buddies what ultimately happened with him. I'd had too many friends come home and self-destruct, and I really didn't want to hear that another name had been added to the list.

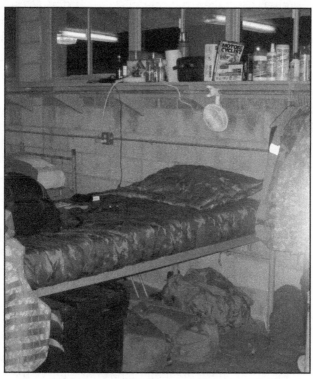

Skintag's empty hootch.

19

DEATHWISH

I t is hard to be a leader of any sort. It is even harder to be a leader of men at war, when the consequences of your actions are life-and-death. Because of these high stakes, every action you take will be highly scrutinized by the men you lead and by your leaders who evaluate your performance. It's a zero-defect situation.

A baseball player can bat .300 for a year and consider it a success. A gambler can win 51 percent of his bets and be successful. But a combat leader can run one hundred combat missions, and if ninety-nine are flawless he is still a failure. When he makes that one mistake, and as a result his men die or his mission fails, he will only be remembered for the screwup. All the good he did before will be forgotten, and his legacy will be one of failure. In combat, a 99-percent success rate is just not good enough.

Given this impossible standard of success, it is easy for soldiers to snipe at their commanders, but it's not always a fair thing to do. The fact is that everyone screws up at one point or another in combat, but when an error is made the focus is never on the dozens of grunts in action. The focus is on the commander, the leader, the man in charge, and it rarely flows downstream to a lower-ranking dude. It's the man at the top who gets the blame assigned when the final after-action reports are drawn up. Simply put, every officer is taught on day one that as commander, they are responsible for all the things their unit accomplishes, and is to blame for all the things their unit fails to accomplish.

The weight of command is heavy, and all are not suited for it. Some people make great privates, but wouldn't last a day in command. And there are some commanders who should have never been promoted above the rank of private, because they don't have the mettle, the character, or the common sense to lead men in combat. This is a story about a man who comes from the latter group: An officer who should have been never left the rank of private. His name is Deathwish.

The ironic thing about Deathwish's story is that his infamous nom-de-guerre nickname is misleading, and requires a brief explanation. On the surface, Deathwish implies that he was out in the thick of things, trying to get himself killed in order to garner some awards or medals and a heroic legacy back home. None of these conclusions would be true. To the contrary, Deathwish was firmly against anyone, including himself, getting awards or medals. He had no interest in being seen as a hero, and he was looking forward to retirement when he got home from the war, not a parade in his honor.

If his nickname were to reflect his actual attitudes about himself, a better moniker would have been "Lifewish," because he made it a point to remind us regularly that he wasn't going to get hurt over there. Time after time he would lecture us on how poor the enemy was in combat, and how they didn't have the skills nor the weapons to harm us. No, the name Deathwish was a nickname of projection, of how he made *us* feel. Death was what he projected onto us, a hot potato that, judging by the way he planned our missions, he was always happy to toss into our laps. His flippant dismissal of our critiques of his half-assed and aloof planning made us feel like he wanted us dead. And his childish assertions that everything would be okay could only be explained by his secretly wanting us to die.

In the morning admin meetings, when Deathwish would pick his sacrificial lambs for the day's mission, we would all cringe when we heard our names spoken aloud. We would be sweating it out from that moment until we were lucky enough to return home later that day from our risk-filled assignment.

But Deathwish never broke a sweat in combat, because of his confidence that the enemy were poor soldiers and couldn't hit a barn if they were shooting at it from twenty meters away. He was cocky in this belief to the point of arrogance, blithely assured that nothing bad was going to happen to him.

Despite the fact that time and time again we clawed out of Taliban ambushes like a rabbit chewing its leg off to escape a snare, he never took our suggestions to improve the planning or manning of the missions he assigned. He showed no creativity, and just kept repeating the same unimaginative patrols in the same areas with minimal gunpower over and over again.

I can remember him telling me, after returning from another one of his poorly planned near-death encounters, that I shouldn't complain. I told him we needed more guys on the mission. I told him we needed to stop leaving the FOB at the same time each day. I told him we needed to plan better for the contingencies we encountered. He smirked dismissively, and said, "What's the problem, you made it back alive today, didn't you?"

And therein lays the rub, the key to why he was such a horrible leader: It was all about *him*. It wasn't about the men he led or their welfare. It was about his personal conviction that he was a sound tactical planner, and that he was going to make it home fine, and we should stand firmly in the light of his brilliance and share his confidence. It was this tactical brilliance that allowed him to cut corners and shoot us willy-nilly into the wind.

If these conclusions seem too emotional, and these statements seem too harsh, let me share some other perspectives on Deathwish from my unit teammates who also feel the same way about him. These are direct quotes my unit buddies remember coming directly from the mouth of Deathwish himself:

"You're all expendable."

"A good leader has to lose some soldiers"

"Don't worry, you have life insurance."

Thinking back to the first day I met Deathwish, he seemed like a nice enough guy who I looked forward to serving under. He led a convoy to pick me up from our corps HQ, as I had just arrived in country and had been assigned to his unit in Ghazni. Off the top, I liked him because I could tell he was educated, bright, and laid-back.

We shared a common hootch for the first week, as permanent housing on this FOB had yet to be assigned. I chuckled to myself when I saw how he organized his space. There was something grandmotherly about how he kept house. He folded his clothing in neat piles, and kept everything organized in an orderly fashion in his wall locker. My stuff, in contrast, was pretty much in constant movement from a large clean lump on my top empty top bunk, to a large dirty lump on the floor.

His living space felt more like a peaceful college dorm room than a soldier's quarters. At first I enjoyed his company, as he liked to debate politics of all sort, which was my favorite pastime when there was nothing going on. But I quickly grew weary of our discussions as he was always convinced he was right in every debate. There was never a moment I can recall him admitting his position was even partially flawed. One never heard Deathwish say, "You know, I never thought of it that way."

Even when he picked a subject that one of his opponents was highly educated on and got schooled in the verbal sparring, he would push his Coke-bottle glasses up high onto the bridge of his nose, and say something dismissive like, "Well, it's clear you just don't understand the issue." That was the sign to change subjects to something more within his comfort zone.

Despite this annoying habit, his stubborn arrogance was easily forgivable. There are lots of blowhards in the Army, and type-A personalities are a dime a dozen in combat arms units like ours. Being a stubborn know-it-all who never wants to lose is, as far as I'm concerned, a forgivable sin. Many of my comrades would likely accuse me of having also committed this transgression.

The first time I saw Deathwish scare me was the first time we were exposed to possible danger. The day started normally, with him neatly folding his sleeping outfit and tucking it away in his wall locker. On this day, the main unit that had lived there for over a year had departed the large, old Russian air base we now called our new home, leaving only about two dozen soldiers behind. Normally there were over four hundred Afghan soldiers permanently stationed to defend it.

To say I was feeling a little vulnerable would be an understatement. We knew that the Taliban was aware that almost all the Afghan soldiers had left the FOB, and that the replacement unit hadn't arrived yet. The FOB could have easily been overrun had the enemy desired to make the effort, so I considered my jitters to be reasonable. Add to this mix that I had only been in country for about four days, and it's safe to say I was pretty much scared shitless. Yet to Deathwish our situation was nothing to even think about. His calm resolve at this dangerous predicament was both reassuring and troubling for me.

Deathwish decided that we would not increase our defensive posture, and instead act as if everything was normal. His wishful thinking was that if we acted like everything was normal, the enemy would be hesitant to attack, and wouldn't hit us. His plan that he briefed to the handful of us at the morning meeting was to casually walk the whole FOB perimeter in a show of confidence to any enemy observers. At the time, the FOB perimeter was nothing more than an eroded dirt berm with rusted Russian barbed wire clumped along its top at random spots. The entire perimeter was pretty large, forming a rectangle about a mile and a half long in its totality. Most of the perimeter was within close range (less than 200 meters) from the mud ruins of houses and walls that surrounded the FOB. It didn't take a genius to determine these abandoned structures, with their windows and spider holes, made perfect sniper hiding spots.

Deathwish briefed the mission that four of us would be making this patrol. Seeing as I was one of the four, I went back to my hootch to put on my body armor, helmet, and other appropriate gear once the briefing ended. I grabbed my rifle and a bunch of extra ammo magazines and a grenade for good measure. This was the standard operating procedure for anyone pulling perimeter security on any FOB in Afghanistan, so I figured it was what was expected of me.

When I met him back at the designated rally point to begin our patrol, Deathwish was there with an interpreter and one other soldier (the Groundskeeper). Neither of them had their rifles. Neither of them had body armor on. The only thing in their hands were coffee cups, and in the case of the Groundskeeper, a lit cigarette. As almost an afterthought, their pistols hung loosely on their hips, holsters snapped shut. Even being the new guy in country, I knew their pea shooters would have been worthless against a Taliban or two with AK-47s at 200 meters.

They looked at me as I walked up to them, then at each other. Their eyes revealed their emotions long before their words did. They clearly thought I was crazy for sporting all my gear and my rifle in the hot midday sun. Then they laughed, and began mocking me for doing what I thought any rational soldier would do: Get geared up and ready to kick Taliban ass.

The Groundskeeper told me to go back and put all my gear back in my hootch. He being an NCO, and me being an officer, I politely refused. They then joked about me being scared and that I needed to relax. I decided to ignore their bad advice, and I kept all my gear on as we began our thankfully uneventful perimeter patrol.

The next time I saw Deathwish show his inability to grasp the severity of the events unfolding around him was on our first combat patrol with actual enemy contact. He was riding in the lead Humvee of our convoy with Deg and the Badger when we all left the FOB, but my vehicle split from his in order to better engage some enemy soldiers who had been scooting around a town south of our FOB. My element was south of Deathwish's Humvee as they drove fleeing enemy soldiers toward our position. The Taliban were being driven toward our position, and we set up a hasty perimeter and waited for their arrival.

Off in the distance, we saw an Afghan National Army pickup truck speeding toward us, with the Humvee straining to keep up. No one in my element was expecting the surprise we got when the pickup got close enough for us to see who was riding in it. In the cargo bed of this lead pickup, whipping his arms in the air like a kid on a roller-coaster ride, was Deathwish. He had no body armor on. His helmet was nowhere in sight, and his short, blondish hair was blowing in the breeze like some kid sitting in front of a fan. The pickup swerved to a stop in front of us, and he hopped off. In my vehicle was a lieutenant colonel who outranked Deathwish and immediately jacked him up for not having on his proper protective gear. Deathwish started to offer up some crazy explanation as to why he had to ditch it all, but it wasn't winning any points with the colonel.

I don't want to be around two senior ranking officers when they are arguing, so I slinked over to Deg and Badger. They were equally incredulous at Deathwish's antics. Deg pulled the cigarette from his mouth, stared at the ground kicking small dust piles, and offered up these prophetic words: "Sad thing is that it's the asshole that never gets a scratch, and causes good soldiers to die."

Bubba, one of our teammates, had been lucky enough to escape our unit by arranging a transfer to another FOB. He had literally developed ulcers from the stress of Deathwish's missions and asked me the day before he was transferred, with a total sense of seriousness: "Is he trying to kill us?"

Since our unit was small and isolated, there wasn't anyone to put Deathwish in check. The other American FOB close by, which did have a couple of senior ranking officers, felt the same way about him as we did, but Deathwish wasn't in their chain of command, so they were powerless to curb his bad behavior. This other FOB had developed their own nickname for him, and called him "Ass Clown."

My buddy Ski had a chance to rid us once and for all of the problem of Deathwish. Our hatred and fear of Deathwish had gotten to a point that we wanted him gone. We all had too many poorly planned and undermanned missions from him under our belt. We all had moments when he had said or done something that made us want to choke him out. My point of no return was when Ski and I were surrounded by Taliban, and while I was desperately trying to give Deathwish our grid coordinates on the radio, an RPG exploded near our position. Deathwish heard the blast on his end of the radio, and asked "Is that an RPG?" I screamed "*Yes!* And they are getting closer." He began to chuckle. I could literally hear him over the radio laughing at our predicament. Yeah, it's fair to say that by this point most of us were ready to mutiny.

So when the day of reckoning came and Ski had a chance to get rid of Deathwish, we were all being ambushed and were taking fire from two sides from Taliban fighters with small arms and rocket propelled grenades. Deathwish had decided to lead this mission, and was present for the festivities. When I drove our Humvee into the fray to help rescue some wounded soldiers who were in the middle of the ambush, there in front of us was Deathwish.

He had abandoned his vehicle, and stood in no-man's-land, literally spinning around in the mud like a ballerina. It was like he was in some sort of trance, as he whirled around, slipping and sliding, pointing in all directions. Any orders or commands he was issuing were drowned out by gunfire and explosions. His mouth was moving, but none of us could hear anything he said. He was in the geographic middle of the ambush, with both sides firing around him, and seemed oblivious to this dangerous fact.

I kept hearing Ski, who was shooting our M240 Bravo machine gun, screaming at Deathwish to "Get the fuck out of the way!" Deathwish was directly in Ski's line of sight to the enemy fighters, and Ski had to withhold easy kill shots because they would have likely also hit Deathwish. To this day, Ski will honestly tell you he regrets not taking those shots. He shares my belief that the net positives would have exceeded the negatives had he dropped Deathwish and the Taliban soldiers.

To this day, I hate Deathwish more than I hate any Taliban I ever fought in Afghanistan.

PART 2:

HOOTCH POLITICS

A civilian primer on the term hootch: The origin of the American military slang term hootch (hootches, plural) is uncertain. Some suggest that it originates from the Japanese word uchi, meaning "house" or "hut." If this is the case, then the Army use of the term hootch could date back to the Pacific theater of World War II. But it is undeniable that the term came to its height of popularity during the Vietnam war, when American GIs used it to refer to their living quarters, and also to the simple civilian dwellings of the Vietnamese people.

The term hootch spawned other related slang words and terms. For some GIs, a hootch wasn't complete if it didn't have a "hootchie girl" (a local woman who served as a prostitute/house maid). Today, almost forty years after Vietnam, the term hootch remains in regular usage by soldiers in the U.S. Army, especially in austere and underdeveloped places like Afghanistan.

When it comes to the American public's feelings about their soldiers, my experience is that our society is broken into two major competing camps. There are those that worship the warrior, and forgive him any and all indiscretions. They will defend our excesses and abuses to the end.

And on the other hand, there are those that, due to their objections to war or the objections to a particular war, will find the American warrior always at fault, tainted by his or her participation in an unpopular or unjust war. This group is quick to judge in an unfavorable light the soldier and his or her actions no matter what the circumstances.

The truth as I see it, as evidenced by my own good and bad actions and habits as a soldier, usually lies somewhere in between these two extreme positions. The soldier does not operate in a black-and-white world, so to romanticize or demonize both miss the target. The soldier is the fusion of Christ and Judas, the wolf and the sheep, and the aggressor and the victim. We are capable of altruism and moral failure at any given moment on any given day.

Soldiers recognize this fact perhaps better than anyone, but that doesn't mean they agree on what constitutes altruism and moral failures. Soldiers who serve in the same army, under the same flag, and in the same uniform, will interpret their actions and justifications in starkly different ways.

Soldiers, much like civil society, are also divided into camps of liberals, conservatives, realists, and pragmatists. Soldiers, sometimes intentionally and sometimes accidentally, form factions within their units and act accordingly to shape soldier culture, how they live their daily lives at war, and even influencing how they and their immediate leaders prosecute the fight. Let me return to the movie *Platoon* for a good cinematic example of this faction-formation process. In the movie, the infantry platoon was divided into two groups. There were those who followed Barnes, the coldhearted realist, and those who followed Elias, the compassionate humanist. The result in the movie, as well as in the two special units I served with in Afghanistan, is a constant simmering battle for the soul of the group.

Unlike *Platoon*, our conflicts never boiled over into fratricidal actions We kept the political conflicts among our team at a low boil. We never lost sight of who the real enemy was: The guys in the turbans trying to kill us. Politics was always a secondary battlefield for us, but this is not always the case, as intentional fratricide over power squabbles or personal conflicts has been a fact of military life forever.

My unit often joked about how well we all got along, living in cramped hootches for a year, given that our sixteen-man group was comprised of fundamentalist Christians and atheists, liberals and conservatives, unrepentant Confederates and Northerners, and perhaps the most difficult conflict to reconcile: hardcore New York Yankees and Boston Red Sox fans.

But it would be a lie to say that there wasn't constant friction between us, which at times got very loud and mean-spirited, and on a couple occasions ended with some pushing and shoving. The categories of conflict that caused these disputes were wide -ranging:

What were the correct tactics to employ in the fight in Afghanistan (conventional war versus counterinsurgency)?

How should we treat the Afghans: as subordinates or equal partners?

Was the humanitarian assistance and FOO money we were giving the Afghans a good thing, or was it retarding their ability to develop and solve their own problems?

How much corruption, if any, was acceptable in the ranks of the Afghan Army, Afghan police, and our own unit in order to make progress against the enemy?

PTSD: was it real, or was it a cop-out by cowardly soldiers?

Religious tolerance: how far should we go in acceptance of other viewpoints and faiths?

And lastly, the most contentious issue of them all, the one that caused the most disgust and debate, and the one that brought the strongest rebuke from back home: was it okay to shoot Afghan cats and dogs for fun and sport?

These and other disputes are worth reviewing to see how hootch politics can unite a unit, as well as divide it.

20

BLOOD SPORT

The most emotional dispute that we had in Afghanistan was the feud between those who killed dogs and cats and those who didn't. This fight was over the simple question of whether it was ethical to shoot innocent animals for sport. Our unit was cut into two clearly defined factions on this matter. One faction was actively involved in either harboring, feeding, and domesticating dogs and cats, while the other group was hunting them and killing them at will.

In effect, one man's newly acquired pet was another man's moving target, which, as you can imagine, made for some harsh words and feelings when you came upon the lifeless, bloody corpse of the puppy you had been training and feeding for weeks, and the bullet hole in its head matched that of a U.S. Army-issued weapon.

In this debate, I was firmly on the side of letting the animals live out their normal existence and not harming them unless they posed an immediate threat to one's personal safety. I had been raised with both cats and dogs, and that no doubt shaped my view on the matter, but I also saw some simple truths that made the blood sport of killing these animals totally unnecessary and unjustifiable in almost every situation.

Had those who killed the dogs and cats been hunting for meat because we were starving, I would have joined them in shooting dogs without hesitation. But this wasn't the case. We may have lacked a proper diet, but we never went hungry. This killing of dogs and cats was done purely for fun, and the excuses offered by the pro-killing faction were frankly threadbare at best.

Those who participated in this blood sport usually claimed that it was valuable target practice. But they could have easily set up traditional targets anywhere and shot at these instead if they really needed practice.

Advocates of dog and cat killing didn't limit themselves to guns and rifles to achieve their goals, which further weakened their argument about needing target practice. They used all means of tools available to kill their victims. A couple guys in our unit made it a point to intentionally swerve into dogs sitting passively by the side of the road as our Humvee convoys rolled past. The dogs were usually left crippled and bloody, but not dead, leaving the Afghans responsible for cleaning up the mess.

Falcon was perhaps the most active dog and cat hunter. He liked to show off an infamous picture of himself, holding his crossbow in one hand, and a kitten impaled through the head on the end of a crossbow bolt in his other hand. As I remember the story, he had been after this kitten for a couple days, because it had been poking around the door of his hootch looking for food and warmth. He was able to get a close-range crossbow shot through its unsuspecting head one morning, and the proud photographic evidence remains to this day of his trophy kill. Spanky liked to boast of the longest kill of a small puppy he wasted at over 600 yards with his M4 rifle. And the Greek was proud of the impressive body count he had racked up after a day of shooting dogs at the trash dump outside the walls of our FOB.

If you talked to the advocates of the killing, you could tell they did it mostly for the fun and the thrill of exercising their shooting prowess. It was sport, pure and simple. There was no ethical or moral issue for them; these were just dirty dogs and cats with no intrinsic value to their world. If you attacked this logic and accused them of doing wrong, they would switch gears and argue that it was really being done for health and sanitation reasons. The dogs were overpopulated, malnourished, and full of disease, so it was humane to thin the herd. I would often listen to this rationalization, and counterpropose that that the Afghan people were also overpopulated, malnourished, and full of disease. Should we be indiscriminately thinning their population too?

One fact that they could argue in their defense, which was indisputable, was that Afghans also had a high disregard for dogs, and treated them with a cruelty and disrespect that made dog-fighting NFL quarterback Michael Vick look like an SPCA board member when it came to dealing with man's best friend. For some, it was fine for us to abuse dogs and cats because it was the social norm of Afghan culture. With the exception of the famed Afghan Hounds, known as *tazis*, Afghan dogs were constantly beaten, yelled at, and chased off as they wandered the streets looking for food. There was no petting of dogs in Afghanistan, and most dogs were feral and fending for themselves. Many dogs died every day of starvation, malnourishment, parasites, and beatings well before my buddies could put them in their rifle's crosshairs.

The *tazis*, who were the exception to this neglect, were not nomads on the Afghan landscape, but in fact were highly prized and valuable possessions. On a lark, I began taking pictures of these dogs throughout my tour, and sent them via e-mail to a group of Afghan hound breeders back home who I thought would be interested in seeing these dogs in their natural environment. I was quickly bombarded with e-mail inquiries from across the globe. It turns out that no purebred authentic Afghan hounds had been exported from Afghanistan for decades, and breeders were willing to pay top dollar for a true Afghan-born specimen. A woman from Finland e-mailed me after seeing my pictures, and offered thousands of dollars for a *tazi*. I worked with one of my interpreters to try to line up a purchase of a dog for export to her, which was both possible and legal to do.

As testimony to how things work in Afghanistan, within moments of me telling my interpreter that I wished to find and purchase a quality *tazi* specimen, he was on his cell phone to his cousin, who then put in a call to a friend who worked at the Afghan zoo in Kabul. Some quick deals were cut, and this zoo employee was willing and able to steal a purebred *tazi* from the king's family line of hunting hounds, and have it sent to my remote FOB within days. While I could have made a quick and easy killing financially, I nixed the deal because I didn't want to be part of the looting of the country's few remaining historical treasures. I share this vignette only to show that where my buddies saw flea-bitten pests in their gun sites, I saw valuable dogs who to breeders back in the real world, were treasures worth large sums of money.

I can only think of one time in my yearlong tour that some dog killing was justified. There was a large pack of hostile dogs on my first FOB in Ghazni. The base was sparsely populated with only a few American soldiers, but geographically it was large. I would go jogging in the afternoons and would bring a pistol to scare off this unfriendly pack, which at times would muster the courage to chase me. It was ultimately decided that they were a safety risk, so the pack of dogs was culled with pistols and rifles down to a smaller, more manageable size. A pit was dug, and the dozens of dead dogs were dragged into the hole and burned with gasoline. It wasn't pretty, but it wasn't done out of cruelty or blood sport. There was a real-world reason to do it. The pack was too large and growing more and more aggressive against the humans who also lived there by the day.

I felt another reason why we should make it a point to treat animals humanely was because it was a great opportunity to show the Afghans a progressive and more modern way to treat other living creatures. The American military went out of its way to tout its advances in racial unity, setting an example to the tribal and ethnically adverse Afghan society. They were still dealing with serious tribal and ethnic problems, and our ability to have a melting-pot army showed that it was an achievable goal for them too. On the gender front, we also used our progressive inclusion of women at all ranks to showcase their need to make advances in the inclusion of women. Our female soldiers wielded a lot of clout, compared to their women who were usually locked behind walls with few civil rights.

In my year in Afghanistan, I would say that my small unit killed over two hundred dogs and about a dozen cats. With the exception of that one dog-culling operation for the sake of safety, every one of these kills was an intentional act with no justification beyond those offered by the shooters. Those of us who were against this cruelty would spend evenings in our hootches railing against what we saw as unnecessary acts of brutality, but in the end we were powerless to stop it because the perpetrators were of equal or greater rank than its opponents. If there was any official rule or regulation prohibiting these shootings, I never heard of it. I think it ultimately was up to the commander's discretion in his area of operations, and in my case, our commanders didn't seem to have a problem with it.

I do remember on our first week in country, the corps commander gave us a briefing on what to expect in the eastern part of the country. Tucked somewhere in the middle of his brief was a warning about what he didn't want to see us do: "Don't let me catch you abusing any dogs out there."

At the time we had no clue as to what he was referring to. Was he talking about dogs? No one had ever mentioned dogs before in three months of mobilization training. Frankly, I think we were more concerned with the two-legged creatures walking around (Taliban) to have thought much about the four-legged variety. Was "dogs" his euphemism for Afghan civilians? Was it a warning not to torture captured Taliban? Or was he just a big animal lover sharing his personal concern for Fido and Spot? We weren't sure at the time, so we all just nodded in agreement. Apparently, his warning was based on the fact that dog killing is a common sport in Afghanistan among soldiers, and we were not the first unit to hit the dog population hard. And unfortunately, we won't be the last group of soldiers who feel dogs and cats are fair game in Afghanistan.

Target practice on the "dog range."

Purebred Afghan hounds wandering around a village. Despite the claims of the dog hunters, these animals were highly trained sight hounds, and would sell for thousands of dollars back in the United States.

21

PATCH NAZIS

Perhaps the most trivial dispute during our tour was also the one that garnered the most harassment from higher HQ: The choice and wear of combat patches. On one fateful night it even involved a showdown with the command sergeant major of our brigade, when he bulldogged the Falcon for wearing an "improper" combat patch, and demanded that it be removed on the spot. Even though the Falcon was able to cite regulation showing he was right, no one wins in a fight with the brigade's senior NCO.

The never-ending debate over combat patches was a default topic to fight about when nothing else was going on. It was both a meaningless issue and one that struck a note of honor and pride that combat soldiers felt they earned and that needed to be defended.

Combat patches are a symbol of pride to any soldier. The derogatory term of "slick sleeve" is used to describe someone who hasn't earned a combat patch yet. Having a combat patch instantly separates one from the combat-zone virgins who have never been in harm's way.

Once a soldier has been in a combat theater for more than thirty days, he or she is authorized to wear a combat patch on their right sleeve. It is officially referred to in Army regulations as an SSI-FWTS, which stands for *shoulder sleeve insignia-former wartime service*. The regulation's language is pretty clear. The regulation allows for the wear of your unit patch, or your higher echelon unit's patch, on the right sleeve for those who served in a combat zone for thirty days or more.

However, people interpret what exactly is authorized differently, based on their own understanding of the regulation. We had one clueless high-ranking officer (Deathwish) who insisted we were not authorized to wear any combat patch until the completion of our yearlong tour, even though the regulation clearly stated that thirty days was enough time to begin wearing a combat patch.

So for a period of time on FOB Ghazni, after our thirty days in country, we spent hours griping and bitching about Deathwish's refusal to sport this badge of honor. We were the only unit in the country that was still walking around slick-sleeved, and it made us feel like we were stuck on in the freshman class when we knew we had graduated to up-perclassmen. On some days, we would get some razzing from other U.S. units we had joint operations with, and the result would be hours spent griping about Deathwish and his dicked-up patch policy.

Eventually, Deathwish's reign of error was overruled by a higher authority in our chain of command (likely the result of someone in our unit ratting him out), and we were finally allowed to put on the combat patch of our brigade, but *only* the patch of the brigade. This was only a partial victory. As per regulation, we should have also been authorized the choice to wear either the brigade patch or our higher HQ's patch.

Pretty much to the man, we wanted to wear the patch of our higher headquarters, the 10th Mountain Division, be-cause frankly our little no-name National Guard brigade was doing a terrible job supporting us, and the 10th Mountain was always there to help us out. We felt a lot more like members of the 10th than we did our own home brigade. On a more petty and trivial level, we wanted the 10th Mountain patch because it was cooler. Why drive a 1994 Ford Taurus when you can be seen cruising around town in new Range Rover? The 10th Mountain patch was the Range Rover of combat patches, a symbol that says "Been there, done that!" from Afghanistan all the way back to kicking Nazi ass in Europe.

The 10th Mountain patch was identified among all Army ranks as a tough, war-fighting unit. The obscure Na-tional Guard brigade's patch that we had been given the okay to wear was an unknown unit that frankly no one recognized or had seen outside of its home state. The most common reaction to this lesser brigade patch was to be asked if was an ice cream cone, as it was shaped like a scoop of vanilla.

We had received an official memorandum from the 10th Mountain Division allowing us to wear their combat patch, in recognition for the numerous missions we had jointly conducted with various elements from their division. But Deathwish arbitrarily decided we couldn't wear the 10th Mountain patch for reasons that never made much sense. When it came down to it, we all knew it was silly to waste time fighting over patches, but type-A personalities like to argue over dumb stuff, and the last thing we wanted to do was die out on mission wearing a patch that looked like an ad for Baskin-Robbins 33 flavors.

So, being the independent and rebellious operators that we were, we ran a silly game of covert patch switching. On the FOB, under the watchful eyes of patch Nazi Deathwish, we wore the ice cream patch. But the minute we left the FOB, we tore off the Velcro patches and replaced them with our preferred 10th Mountain patches. When we would return, we would reverse the switch and be back in line with patch Nazi doctrine.

Guys like me, Falcon, Casanova, and the Greek were strong advocates of the freedom to choose your combat patch from the authorized choices. Others, like Badger and Mr. OCD, either didn't care or disagreed with going against our leader's arbitrary limitation of our rightful choices.

Another battlefield of the patch conflict was the unauthorized "morale patches," as they are informally known. These were patches worn by irregular units, usually the Special Forces, which were homemade and comical. Morale patches could be made up at Bagram in about a day at the seamstress shop. You would give the Filipino and Indian sewers your design, and they would crank out a patch for you for a few bucks. Some of the more popular ones were the tab worn above the Mountain tab of the 10th Mountain Division. The tab said *Broke Back*, and when worn in conjunction with the regulation 10th Mountain patch, would read *Broke Back Mountain*. Other popular tabs were *Infidel, Team*

America and *Fuck Yeah*. The last two were made popular by the theme song from the cult classic, war-on-terror spoof movie *Team America*.

I had a few unique morale patches made up on my own. One said *I love Hazaras*, which was in reference to the ethnic tribe in Afghanistan who were the best soldiers, and the most anti-Taliban community in the country (given the fact that the Taliban, when in power, had committed a nationwide ethnic-cleansing campaign of mass murder of the Hazara people). Unfortunately, Hazaras were widely discriminated against, and anyone who has read *The Kite Runner* is intimately familiar with how Hazaras were treated by the other majority tribes in Afghanistan.

One afternoon I had the opportunity to hang out in the transient hootches in Kabul, where soldiers who were moving from one FOB to another usually ended up for a couple days. I met up with two Afghan interpreters who had been injured in an IED strike and were assigned to the same transient hootch as I was. They were both Pashtun, and in the course of our friendly but rambling conversation, they said something derogatory against the Hazara people. Having worked for months with some great Hazara soldiers and villagers, I took offense to this comment and spoke up on their behalf. This immediately opened up a mean-spirited verbal fight that made these Afghan interpreters seem a lot like pro-segregation Southerners in the 1950s. I was so frustrated at their blatant racism, I ran over to the seamstress shop on post and had them make me up the *I Love Hazaras* tab, which I proudly wore on my boonie cap. When I returned to the hootches, the two Pashtun interpreters were enraged to the point that one stormed out of the hootch, clutching his gauze dressing that was loosely wrapped around his belly wound. He was so outraged by my statement of support for the Hazara people, he never returned to the hootch. So much for ethnic reconciliation.

Since our unit was small and working mostly with Afghans, we didn't have too much adult supervision from higher headquarters, so we were able to wear these unauthorized patches a lot. As long as Deathwish didn't see them, we were good to go. Once he caught me with a morale tab on, and he grounded me from a mission for refusing to remove it. He approached me as I was lining up vehicles for an emergency mission to go assist some Afghan national police who were under siege, and grabbed my body armor and attempted to rip the *Team America* patch off my body armor. I grabbed his arm and pushed him away, surprised that he was picking that moment when soldiers were about to go out into harm's way on an in-extremis mission, to fight over patches. He was flabbergasted at my reaction and defiance, and told me I couldn't go out on the mission as punishment. I was sent back to the TOC and told to report to the commander, which I did. I explained what had happened, and I stood my ground that it was a long-standing Army tradition to not put hands on another soldier. It was one thing to give an order to do something; it was another thing to use force to accomplish it. Had Deathwish locked me up and told me to remove it, I would have complied, then put the patch back on once I left the FOB. But he never did that, he just grabbed at me, and I responded properly by refusing to follow his order.

Later that day, I was told by our commander that I was wrong to wear the patch, but that Deathwish was wrong to lay hands on me. It ended up as a tie. No harm, no foul so to speak, and I never got in any further trouble over the incident. Deathwish was clearly hoping for some kind of punishment for me, but it never came. And in his twisted sense of right and wrong, the punishment he "inflicted" on me (by removing me from the mission) only resulted in the guys going out without another set of eyes and trigger fingers, which in effect was a punishment on them. So as you can see, even something as trivial as patches played an important and controversial role in our lives at war.

22

BLOGGING

The craft of telling stories from the battlefield goes back to the writers of antiquity. War is so intense and stimulates such emotions, that despite its tragic outcomes it generates perhaps more written pages than any other subject in human existence. And the readers, who know the ending is always bloody, still pursue war writings with a morbid curiosity that never seems to be satiated.

Thanks to the Internet and blogging, today's war stories come in hot and fast. There are rarely any censors nor editors that stand between you the reader and the soldier sharing his or her experiences fresh from the battlefield. Through this new art form of blogging, the world has perhaps the timeliest, sincerest, and unfiltered look at what life is like at war.

Our unit had a couple active and regular bloggers, mainly me and the Falcon. We wrote for different reasons and to a different audience, but nonetheless we wrote because we had stories and information we wanted to share, and arguments we wanted to make, and attention we wanted drawn to the difficult war being fought by U.S. servicemen and women in Afghanistan.

Despite the fact that the two of us, along with the overwhelming majority of all bloggers military wide, portrayed the war and the soldiers in it favorably, there are a lot of members in today's military who frown on the blogger and who remain adversarial to bloggers trying to tell their war stories.

These critics dwell at all levels of command in the Army, and oppose blogging for different reasons. Higher levels of command, which are used to shaping information and controlling its distribution, are now confronted with a world where every low-ranking grunt with an ax to grind can deliver his message to a global audience, and really screw things up. Too many examples of soldiers posting videos or blogs on the

Internet that portray offensive, immoral, or otherwise stupid actions, have meant a lot of damage-control efforts at the top. I'm reminded of the example of a large, successful operation carried out by the Marines in Iraq. The operation had captured and killed a large number of enemy, yet what made the news back home was the YouTube video, filmed during the operation, of one of these Marines throwing a puppy off a cliff. So as you can see by this example, with thousands of potentially loose cannons out there on the battlefield filming videos and blogging about things that higher has no control over, one can understand why military bloggers are not always embraced as a welcome newcomer by the higher levels of command.

At our small-unit level, isolated from our higher headquarters, the criticisms of blogging came more from our peers, who to varying degrees were either lukewarm supporters of our writings, or harsh .

Many of our critics' core objections to blogging came from the soldier cultural tenet that there is no room for individuality in the military. Being a blogger is seen by these critics as an attempt to be a lone voice, someone "special" who wants to hog the spotlight. If it was boiled down to a bumper sticker, I think these critics would say: "There is no *blog* in *team*."

In today's military culture, we are trained to follow set standards and procedures and work in groups, not make up our own rules as we see fit as individuals. Blogging is threatening to some because it lets an individual wander off the reservation and skirt the limitations and restrictions that regulate our lives in uniform.

A couple guys in my unit really took a personal dislike to anyone who felt like they were special enough to tell their story on the Internet. It's like being a show-off in their view, seeking attention and trying to be some self-proclaimed and unwarranted hero.

And the fact is, even though I am supportive of blogging, these critics have a reason to be skeptical. There are a lot of fobbits over in Afghanistan and Iraq whose rear-echelon job or location in the country resulted in an uneventful tour (i.e., no combat action). As a result, these fobbits embellish a lot of their experiences to the point that they are in part or completely fictitious. And sure enough, some of these blowhard fakers end up writing fictitious blogs about the battles they never fought and enemies they never shot. Everyone in the Army knows someone who fits this description. A good war story is one that is earned, and these guys never got the chance to earn such stories, so to compensate they make some up, and that really pisses off us dudes who actually did dodge bullets for a year.

So whether it's a dislike of those who are seen as being too individualistic and tooting their own horn, or a dislike of those who are prone to a tall tale, a lot of soldiers frown on blogging.

Frankly, my opinion about these critics was that I really didn't care what they thought. I was a prolific blogger who would have written regardless of whether my peers supported it or harassed me for it. I was motivated both in my desire to let people know of the heroic acts and extreme sacrifices being made by my comrades-in-arms. Falcon was the same way. We never thought we were special, we just wanted people to know about the caliber of soldier we had the honor of serving with, and the challenges of the mission we had been asked to accomplish.

I also blogged as a way to deal with the stresses of my job, and it was as much personal therapy to get the bad stuff (combat stress, trauma, drama) out on the keyboard, than it was a desire to get attention. It was an act of purging that gave me some mental peace after violent and dangerous missions. Even if I only had one person reading it, instead of the thousands who regularly followed my postings, I would have still written the same way with the same frequency and motivation.

In the end, I feel bloggers such as myself contributed to, and continue to contribute to, the home front's understanding of our lives and our sacrifices. Honest and unsterilized bloggers play an important role in educating America on the war, and of the myriad of challenges we continue to face in what is the longest conflict our country has ever fought.

This is the patch I received from G. B. Trudeau of *Doonesbury* fame, for my contributions to his milblog site *The Sandbox*, which continues to host a myriad of excellent military bloggers.

23

HUMANITARIAN ASSISTANCE

What was our job in Afghanistan? Were we there to hunt down and kill bad guys in a lethal game of "whack-a-mole," or were we there to assist in the rebuilding of the country, serving as social workers and welfare police facilitating this process? Or was it a mix of both?

The answer to this question wasn't clear at even the highest levels of our command. The first few years of the war concentrated on the whack-a-mole tactics of hunting and killing bad guys. When we were there in 2006 and 2007, the pendulum was swinging to the other extreme of warm and fuzzy nation-building. The result was a lot of independence and creativity by lower-level commanders, who got to tailor their operations toward which angle they were going to take: kill, cuddle, or both.

Our unit, which due to the fact that we were embedded within the Afghan security forces, had an intense exposure to Afghans and even more autonomy to shape our missions to either lethal or constructive ends. This autonomy, not surprisingly, resulted in our unit breaking into two factions: Those who saw the focus as killing bad guys in the short term, and those who saw our role as rebuilding Afghanistan as the only long-term way to defeat the enemy.

I was a vocal leader among the warm and fuzzy advocates, and went to great measures to push this aspect of action in our counterinsurgency mission. Better known in army parlance as H.A., humanitarian assistance was a type of mission that focused on using clothing, food, economic grants, and technical assistance (farming, engineering, veterinarian services) as a weapon to win the hearts and minds of the populace. In turn, as the theory goes, the people would see the advantages of supporting Coalition Forces and the government of Afghanistan, and stop putting their support behind the Taliban and other anti-Coalition militia.

I had support from guys like Casanova, Old Yeller, Badger, and the Preacher. Vocal opponents to warm and fuzzy H.A. focus came from Falcon, Rebel, Spanky, and others.

How one felt about H.A. tied in closely to how one felt about the downtrodden in the world in general. Were people poor and ignorant because they were lazy, and lacked the initiative to lift themselves up by their bootstraps? Or were they poor because they were victims of generational wars, a destroyed economy, and a lack of opportunity? One's answer to this question usually broke down on classic liberal and conservative ideological lines.

Field ordering officer (FOO) money came into play in this debate too. Each month, one of us would be assigned as the FOO and receive 25,000 dollars to spend on improving the living conditions of our FOB and the Afghan soldiers we lived with. Most FOO officers were happy to spend the money on making our lives better, and making the Afghan security forces more efficient and capable in providing security to their people. But some people, when they were assigned as the FOO, took the position that to spend one penny of it was a waste of American taxpayer dollars. The Greek was the best example of this. He would proudly proclaim, whenever he was assigned the job of FOO, that he "wasn't going to spend a penny of it." His personal conservative ideology made his decision not to spend FOO money simple. The way for Afghans to rise up out of their mess was by their own bootstraps, not a handout. Welfare, especially at the expense of the American taxpayer, wasn't going to happen on the Greek's watch.

In principle, even a progressive guy like myself understood his frustration. Every day we saw Afghans steal and misappropriate money and resources for their personal gain, and no one wanted to support this malfeasance. Corruption was universal, and far exceeded any acceptable level Americans could stomach. But the puritanical approach of the Greek and those like him failed to grasp the role corruption played in many third world countries. Corruption, in a place like Afghanistan or Pakistan or India, is the oil that keeps the system's engine running. Government officials, from police to governors, were paid such a small salary that they were forced to squeeze extra out of the people and projects they administered. It was a way of life that has existed for generations, and continues to exist despite the crusade the Greek had launched to rid the land of corruption.

We have corruption in the United States, but it's better hidden. Here in Afghanistan, corruption is in plain view, and it's the lower-level guys who are the most visibly involved. It is offensive for an American to watch an Afghan police officer shake down motorists. It runs against our universally agreed-upon moral compass of how police should behave. But an Afghan cop who doesn't do this won't make enough to feed his family, and would never have taken the job in the first place if these opportunities for small-scale graft didn't exist. It was uncomfortable truths like this that made it hard for people like the Greek to play along with the system, and fueled their distrust and dislike of the Afghan people.

One had to take a big-picture look at the whole enterprise of FOO, H.A., and combat operations, and factor in these different cultural norms and practices when deciding how best to win in Afghanistan. While I had no problem with going after Taliban anywhere and everywhere they presented themselves, I knew that a kinetic, combat-focused, reactive response would result in a forever war in Afghanistan.

Being a student of low-intensity conflict and the causes behind it (usually economically based), I had previously traveled to other countries going through civil wars and revolutions, and in every case the majority of supporters were not ideologically committed, but instead were throwing in their lot with the insurgents because they felt that it would improve their living conditions more so than a corrupt or abusive government could.

And my experiences in Afghanistan told me that this was also the case. I'd say over 90 percent of the people had no interest in the Taliban's fundamentalist ideology. Instead, this overwhelming majority of the Afghan people were willing to give Coalition Forces and the new government of Af-

ghanistan the benefit of the doubt that we had their best in-
terests at heart. But after nine years of a halfhearted funding
of reconstruction efforts, many of these people had lost hope
in our ability to fix things, and were willing to give the Taliban a second look.

In huge swaths of the country, where there are jobs,
economic development, and an absence of violence, people
shun the Taliban and treat Coalition Forces like welcome
guests. Where there is excessive government corruption, ar-
rogant Afghan police forces, and an overly aggressive game
of whack-a-mole being played by Uncle Sam (with a large
tally of accidental civilian deaths), the Taliban sales pitch
makes a lot more sense, and the people side with the insurgents far more than we would like to see.

Where I was stationed in Paktika Province during the
second half of my tour, there was an extreme lack of economic development. Harsh poverty was the norm, and with
the onset of winter (which meant a virtual cessation of fighting), I saw a window of opportunity to safely and aggressively
win some hearts and minds in the area.

Official H.A. missions (using U.S. government– purchased and delivered food stuffs, clothing, and school items)
were infrequent and rare. In the first six months I had spent
in country in Ghazni, I only participated in two such missions. They were powerful successes, providing goods to
hundreds of civilians and winning lots of goodwill and juicy
intel tidbits, but despite this they did not seem to be the prior-
ity of our higher commanders.

Through the magic of my blog and the internet, I was
able to launch a DIY campaign to collect literally hundreds of
boxes of winter clothing, toys, and school-supply donations
from back home. These mountains of boxes were mailed to
our FOB, where we sorted them out and prepped them for
direct delivery to remote and depressed villages in our area.

At this time, Mr. OCD was our operations officer, so I
would go to his hootch whenever the goodwill boxes were
overflowing out of our storage area, and plead for him to
put together an H.A. mission to a local village. I randomly

picked a village and within a couple days a convoy of Humvees and Afghan National Army trucks would head out and play Santa Claus to a couple hundred impoverished civilians. We didn't rely on higher headquarters for supplies, nor did we ask them permission. We just did it. It was so easy even an infantry officer could do it.

I wasn't alone in these unofficial H.A. efforts. Individual soldiers from all corners of the country were doing the same informal H.A. campaigns. It was just a drop in the bucket in comparison to the might the U.S. Army could have brought into play with their warehouses filled with H.A. supplies, but it was still winning hearts and minds among the Afghan people.

One of the reasons why big Army wasn't jumping in with two feet in support of these types of missions was that the Army runs on statistics and matrices and results. When you kill bad guys, you can count heads. When you pass out H.A., you don't have a concrete measurable stat to show that it was in fact helping to win the war.

It was rational to assume that the show of goodwill would cast our role in a better light for Afghan civilians who were on the fence as to which side to support, but it was hard to prove.

We knew the Taliban went through these same villages and lectured these same people about our desires to destroy their culture, their religion, and to enslave them in nefarious ways. But when we came to their villages, bearing gifts and messages of friendship and cooperation, it put a crimp in the Taliban's message. But how does one measure this crimp in the Taliban's recruiting campaign?

Absent this stat or matrix, I am still confident there are Afghans that I cannot identify, nor count, nor quantify in any measure, who as a result of our H.A. missions of goodwill, decided not to help the Taliban plant an IED, or feed Taliban fighters, or join their cause. But because I can't show my brigade commander a PowerPoint slide with names on it of Afghans who said no to the Taliban as a result of our H.A., it made it all the more difficult to pitch H.A. campaigns to higher headquarters. In the end, today's Army lives and dies on statistics and matrices and PowerPoint slides, and until the impact of H.A. can be quantified, it will remain a lesser-used weapon in our arsenal to defeat the Taliban.

This defense of H.A. operations is not aiming to suggest that H.A. is perfect and without flaws. Critics of H.A., like the Greek, would point out that some of our aid probably ends up in enemy hands. Some soldiers would go even further and launch into borderline racist arguments that the Afghans were lazy, stupid, and didn't deserve any handouts from the hardworking and wholesome members of the Western world. These types weren't too interested in cross-cultural understanding, nor bonding with a foreign people even if it meant helping to win the war.

Another group of soldiers just didn't like going outside the wire on what they saw as unnecessary missions that only put us in harm's way, and had nothing to do with killing Taliban. I remember Rebel asking me why I wanted to plan H.A. missions which, in his opinion served only one goal: To give the enemy free potshots at us.

Another guy in my unit, Fieldmouse, would begrudgingly go out on H.A. missions, but made it clear he didn't support the concept of playing nice with Afghans. He was normally a machine gunner up in the Humvee turret, and he would make it a point to throw toys at kids with the intent of pegging them in the head, as opposed to a gentle toss of a Care Bear or doll for some little girl to catch. Candy, water bottles, and toys were regularly thrown with anger by Fieldmouse rather than as offerings of friendship.

My answer to this range of critics who didn't buy into the whole H.A. mission concept was this: In order to win in Afghanistan (which is a goal both sides of the H.A. debate agreed on), shooting bad guys was only a small fraction of the work that needed to be done. I feel vindicated that today, the highest levels of command, as well as the counterinsurgency think-tankers out there in the United States and UK, have come down hard in favor of the H.A. approach to fighting and winning in Afghanistan. The pendulum is clearly swinging in this direction toward a hearts and mind approach. So much so that in 2009 a Marine general, issued guidance to his merry band of killers that he would rather see Taliban soldiers escape from combat than see innocent civilians die in the process of killing them. His instructions to the thousands of Marines under his command was that their focus is to protect the Afghan populace from the Taliban, allowing local governance and development to bear fruit, as opposed to the game of whack-a-mole and search and destroy. This is a radical change in how the war is being handled from the early years after 2001. But after years of focusing solely on killing the enemy, is it too late to for H.A. to make a difference?

Only time will tell.

Three children smile as they receive free boots, winter clothing, and toys during one of my H.A. missions made possible by donations from supporters back home.

Afghanistan is officially an Islamic nation. The United States Army, as well as most of the Coalition Forces serving there, come from Western, liberal democracies that have a strong Judeo-Christian heritage. Simply put, the two brands of faith don't mix particularly well. As a result, American forces were prohibited from doing any religious agitation, recruitment, or evangelizing by general order 1-bravo (which will be discussed in depth later in this book).

Despite this tinderbox-subject of religion, our unit had many opportunities to share religious beliefs and debate the merits of the competing faiths with our Afghan counterparts.

Like all of the factional debates and fissures we experienced, in the end we kept it pretty friendly, because we were all on the same team fighting a common enemy. Given this fact, Christians, Jews, and even a few atheists like me, were able to work cordially and professionally with Muslim Afghan security forces despite our deeply held differences in god mythology.

The biggest surprise for me, which ran counter to the prevailing myth of the intolerant and uber-fundamentalist Muslims, was that the Afghans tended to be more tolerant and accepting of other belief systems than the Christians I served with. In part this is owed to the fact that the Muslim faith accepts Jesus Christ as a prophet of God, a holy man to be respected and admired, but (and this is an important *but*), he was not the final prophet. According to the Koran, Muhammad was the final arbiter of God's revelations to man. Many Christians are unaware of the fact that Jesus plays a part in the Islamic mythology. I can't think of one time I ever heard an Afghan say anything negative about Christianity or Jesus Christ.

On the other hand, many of the American soldiers who were vocal about their Christian faith were extremely judgmental about the Afghans' Muslim faith, as well as my lack of any religious faith. They ridiculed it, and it was normal to hear some of the guys tell the Afghan soldiers and interpreters that in accordance with their Christian mythology, they were going to hell.

The religious tolerance faction, espoused by guys like Dexter, Rainbow, Fidel, and Casanova, was at stark odds with guys like the Falcon and Spanky and Rebel. I was usually the odd man out, being the lone atheist in the bunch.

Afghans as a group weren't into evangelizing their belief system to outside people (internally, within their culture, the opposite seemed to be the case, as they were hyper-vigilant enforcers of Islam). From an outsider's point of view, the Afghans had been taught things that were almost comical. I had well-versed interpreters tell me that in every library in America, the Koran is on the highest shelf in the library as a sign of respect for its superiority over all other books. I explained to them that this wasn't the case, as I had been in plenty of libraries across the country and the Koran was kept among all other religious texts. Its location was determined more by alphabetical order than religious superiority. They refused to believe my rebuttal of their allegations.

Things like this revealed a lot about Afghanistan's fundamentalist tendency, and the challenges that face their country—or any country, for that matter—that is governed not by rational thought but by religious decrees and mythology. In Afghanistan, there is no exposure to other belief systems. There is no liberal arts education that explores the value and contributions of all belief systems (or even a lack of belief system). Even within Christianity, there are many different schisms and churches that jockey for position with competing interpretations of the Holy Bible. Some Christian sects are very liberal and progressive, while others are ultra-conservative. The result is that the average Christian American is exposed to competing interpretations of what it means to be Christian.

In Afghanistan, there are two Islamic traditions, the Shiite and the Sunni, and they are both very fundamentalist in their teachings and practice. When disputes arose between the two sects, the way they settled their differences was usually though violent rampages against each other. Discussion and debate about their faith was unlikely, and acknowledging that the other side may be right was tantamount to heresy. Those who were willing to consider an opposing viewpoint rarely spoke up about it, because people who did got stoned to death.

So one of the good things about the American presence in Afghanistan is that perhaps for the first time in a generation, foreign people are there challenging Afghans to take a second look at some of the arbitrary and backwards things they have been taught are a part of their faith. Without asking them to give up their faith, like the Russians did thirty years ago, Westerners are showing Afghans that there doesn't have to be a contradiction between embracing modernity and retaining their religious faith.

25

PTSD

There are still people who question whether post-traumatic stress disorder (PTSD) is real. Surprisingly, some of them are frontline soldiers. I served with soldiers who suffered from PTSD (as I have), and with soldiers who mocked and ridiculed those of us going through it. I was jokingly called "Captain Prozac" by some of my buddies, and I heard regular ridicule directed toward guys who weren't acting "normal" anymore. There is nothing off limits for a joke or a jibe among combat soldiers. We ripped each other for all sorts of things that in civil society would be off limits. I took it in stride. I still do. And I don't hold a grudge against those who made a mockery of it. As an infantryman, I had thick skin.

It would be hypocritical of me to complain too much, given that I dished it out as thick as I took it in. I was equally guilty of making fun of my buddies for their baldness, being fat, their dysfunctional families, their ugly wives, and their train-wreck girlfriends. I insulted their semi-retarded spelling abilities, their backwards Taliban-esque religious beliefs, and their poor marksmanship skills.

Despite the fact that we would have all died for each other in combat, we all made it a daily part of our routine to take any and every opportunity to verbally rip into each other. It's part of the bonding process of men at war. It's part of the process of thickening our skins to the real mental challenges we would face out on the battlefield. As long as no blood was drawn, these verbal insults were no harm, no foul, and served a purpose to help us manage the constant stress of being at war.

A lot of guys had early onset of PTSD while still in country. I think technically it is called *generalized anxiety disorder,* a technical precursor for PTSD for soldiers. It's the diagnosis doctors and psychologists have to give before they hand out a PTSD diagnosis because one of the requirements for PTSD, according to the *Diagnostic and Statistical Manual of Mental Disorders*, is to have these anxiety symptoms for one month. Up until you hit that month of being screwed up, you only have generalized anxiety disorder. After that month is up, it's game on for a PTSD diagnosis.

Despite the fact that guys like Ski and I called PTSD the "breakfast of champions," we at first kept our problems inside. I didn't share what I was going through with others. I couldn't sleep. I was having twisted Tim Burton movie nightmares. I was hallucinating on the battlefield, seeing my kids running around between the mud huts among the Afghans. It was trippy. It was scary. I knew something was wrong.

One day our commander walked into the tactical operations center and nonchalantly mentioned to the soldiers seated there that there was a mental health specialist visiting the bigger FOB down the road, and anyone interested in going to talk to her should go. There were so many of us who jumped at this opportunity that we filled up two Humvees. Apparently, I wasn't the only one having problems.

The mental health specialist was an Army major who was a social worker, so she wasn't qualified to officially diagnose any ailments. But she had a speedy field test for PTSD that we took, followed up by a one-on-one interview with her. Every one of us left our little chat with the major with an informal diagnosis of either generalized anxiety disorder or PTSD, and we were given an assortment of meds for depression, insomnia, and anxiety by the physician's assistant who normally ran the medical clinic.

The meds I got gave me even worse dreams, so I passed them off to Ski, who didn't visit the social worker that day because he was out on mission. He also had trippy dreams as a result of the meds, so we fed the remaining pills to some mean, wild dogs that had been harassing us out in the back forty of our FOB.

When I arrived at my second FOB for the second half of my tour, the soldiers who had been living there all along had enjoyed a much less stressful environment, with far fewer combat engagements. They had a couple run-ins with IEDs and gunfights, but they were few and far between compared to what I had been through with my first FOB. As a result, most of the guys on this second FOB were not tweaking with PTSD. Spanky, who lived on this FOB for pretty much the whole year, had a full dose of PTSD issues from his previous deployment to Iraq, but he was managing well here in the Afghanistan. So when I arrived with my pharmacy full of meds, he quickly coined the nickname "Captain Barbiturate" and "Captain Prozac" for me.

On my first FOB, the issue of PTSD wasn't up for debate. Almost all of us who had been out on Deathwish's regular missions had it. But on my new, second FOB, it was a different world with better leadership and less shooting. As a result, some guys here like Rebel, the Falcon, and Mr. OCD thought it was a cop-out. They figured I'd been through the same stuff as they had, and they felt fine, so I must have been bluffing to get attention. I'm not sure what their reasoning was, but it was clear I was the butt of a lot of jokes.

So our unit fell into two camps: Those who were suffering from PTSD, and those who thought it was bullshit. A few of the guys who piled on in these group-harassment moments later confided in me privately that they too were having problems. As our tour wound down, we had more experiences with IEDs, and with wounded soldiers, and with treating wounded soldiers. One whispered to me one night that he was suicidal. Another asked to borrow some of my sleeping pills. In the end, I felt somewhat vindicated by events that occurred after we got home. I jumped right into counseling within days of being back Stateside. It's what I needed to do to keep from going off the deep end. And as the months passed, some of the very soldiers who ridiculed PTSD while in Afghanistan were now also going to the VA for counseling, and others were receiving disability for PTSD.

26

GENERAL ORDER 1-BRAVO

The following is an excerpt from general order 1-B, governing U.S. personnel in Afghanistan.

Prohibited Activities:

Purchase, possession, use, or sale of privately owned firearms, ammunition, explosives, or the introduction of these items into the USCENTCOM Area of Responsibility.

Entrance into a Mosque or other site of Islamic religious significance by non-Moslems unless directed to do so by military authorities, required by military necessity, or as part of an official tour conducted with the approval of military authorities and the host nation. This provision may be made more restrictive by Commanders when the local security situation warrants.

Introduction, purchase, possession, sale, transfer, manufacture or consumption of any alcoholic beverage within the countries of Kuwait, Saudi Arabia, Afghanistan, Pakistan, and Iraq. In all other countries of the USCENTCOM AOR, U.S. military and civilian personnel will conform to their respective component restrictions on alcohol, and maintain appropriate deportment by respecting host-nation laws and customs. In order to maintain good order and discipline and ensure optimum readiness, in all locations where alcohol is not prohibited by the General Order, Commanders and unit chiefs are directed to exercise discretion and good judgment in promulgating and enforcing appropriate guidelines and restrictions. Guidelines should recognize that in some countries although alcohol consumption may be legal within certain facilities such as hotels, personnel, upon any consumption, may be presumed to be under the influence upon leaving the facility or upon operating a motor vehicle (e.g., Qatar, UAE). Alcohol consumption guidelines and restrictions should be regularly reviewed to ensure that they are commensurate with current or foreseen operations, threats and host country actions.

Introduction, purchase, possession, use, sale, transfer, manufacture, or consumption of any controlled substances. Prescription drugs must be accompanied by the original prescription label which identifies the prescribing medical facility or authority.

Introduction, purchase, possession, transfer, sale, creation, or display of any pornographic or sexually explicit photograph, video tapes or CDs, movie, drawing, book, magazine, or similar representation. The prohibitions contained in this subparagraph shall not apply to AFRTS broadcasts and commercial videotapes distributed and/ or displayed through AAFES or MWR outlets located within the USCENTCOM Area of Responsibility. This prohibition also shall not apply within the areas exclusively under the jurisdiction of the United States, such as aboard United States Government vessels and aircraft, which shall remain subject to service rules.

Photographing or filming detainees or human casualties, as well as the possession, distribution, transfer, or posting, whether electronically or physically, of visual images depicting detainees or human casualties, except as required for official duties. "Human Casualties" are defined as dead, wounded, or injured human beings, to include separated body parts, organs and biological material, resulting from either combat or non-combat activities. This prohibition does not apply to the possession of such visual images acquired from open media sources (e.g., magazines and newspapers), nor is the distribution of these unaltered images, subject to copyright markings or notices. Additionally, possession and distribution of open media source images is not prohibited if required for official duties. Finally, with their express consent, the photographing and possession of images of wounded personnel while within medical facilities and during periods of recovery is also not prohibited.

Gambling of any kind, including sports pools, lotteries and raffles, unless permitted by host-nation laws and applicable service component regulations.

Removing, possessing, selling, defacing or destroying archeological artifacts or national treasures.

Selling, bartering or exchanging any currency other than at the official host-nation exchange rate.

Adopting as pets or mascots, caring for, or feeding any type of domestic or wild animal.

Proselytizing of any religion, faith, or practice.

General order 1-bravo should have been called "general order zero," because that's the number of soldiers in the Army who adhered to it in its entirety. It's the only topic of regular debate that everyone in my unit was in agreement on: General order 1-bravo was ridiculous.

Better known as "GO-1B" among the grunts in the Army, the order must have made sense to the guys up in the Pentagon who crafted it. The rule was a commonsense attempt to keep us grunts from doing something we were great at: Screwing up.

The threefold purpose of GO-1B, as laid out by the policy makers who crafted it, was to establish rules to maintain the security, health, and welfare of U.S. forces, ensure the highest standards of order, readiness, and discipline, and to promote, improve, and maintain positive relationships with host-nation populations.

Since I left Afghanistan, the rule has been tweaked in minor ways. The most recent version, signed April 19, 2009, now allows non-married soldiers to engage in consensual heterosexual relations, which had previously been banned. But the core rules, as presented previously, remain in full effect.

And despite their good intentions, they remain ignored and violated by even the highest ranking officers serving in Afghanistan. To be clear, we are not a wanton band of Vikings pillaging the land. I would argue that American soldiers adhere to an extremely high and respectful moral code, and time and time again American soldiers hold the ethical high ground in their daily interactions with their military counterparts, civilians, and even the enemy. Be it in combat or in their daily life back in their hootches, American soldiers are a good bunch. But GO-1B just demands too much, and treats grown men like small children, enforcing restrictions that have never been applied to the American fighting man in our history. From Valley Forge to Vietnam, there's been nothing like GO-1B and that's why it is pretty much ignored.

American soldiers act just like their American civilian counterparts back home. Sex, porn, alcohol, and pets are things that permeate our accepted definition of "normal." They are as much a part of our military culture as they are our civilian culture, but under GO-1B they are banned. So when the Army is transplanted into a foreign land with foreign customs, it's hard to expect the average Joe to just give this all up in the name of sensitivity to the host nation.

Some of the more flamboyant violations of this policy are found at the very top of the rank food chain: The forbidden pets and mascots that wander the larger FOBs across the country. Our corps HQ and our command HQ FOBs, run by a high ranking full-bird colonel and the commanding general, both had a couple of mascot dogs that roamed the FOB with full immunity from GO-1B. It wouldn't be abnormal to see either the general or colonel petting his FOB's pooch as he left a staff meeting.

I've already touched upon some of the other regular violations of this policy, like the consumption of alcohol by guys like Casanova and others. Fact is that many Afghans drink, our coalition partners drink, and many if not most American soldiers also choose to sneak an adult beverage here and there. Personally, I never had a sip of alcohol while I served in Afghanistan, but that wasn't because I was a Goody Two-shoes. I missed a swig of Jack Daniel's like it was no one's business. I felt that if we were responsible enough to carry loaded weapons and make life-or-death decisions on a daily basis, we were also responsible enough to manage alcohol intake. I followed the rule because I never wanted to be impaired if an emergency arose. There was beer and whiskey and brandy around me all the time, but it just wasn't something I was interested in, given the unpredictable nature of Taliban activity in our neighborhood.

Other facets of GO-1B were also regularly ignored. Many of us had privately owned weapons, like captured AK-47s that we took from the enemy as backup rifles to our M-4s. Some guys had sawed-off shotguns that looked like they had been around since before gunpowder was invented. We were at war, and the more weapons we could strap to our bodies or have handy in our vehicles only increased our sense of security. Yet it was technically illegal under GO-1B.

A more controversial violation of GO-1B was the taking of photos of enemy dead. It was commonly done for different reasons. It's a very intimate act to be in combat with a fellow living and breathing human being, and if you are lucky enough to be the victor in that deadly interaction, it's only normal to want to have some type of record of it. Hunters take pictures posing next to their conquered prey. Some even hang the heads of their conquered prey on their living room walls. Soldiers also have that same impulse to display their kills.

I wouldn't support mounting the turban-adorned head of a Taliban on your living room wall, but a lot of guys have violated GO-1B by posting photos on public Web pages, displaying their dead opponents. But I do think we have the right to take personal pictures of the events and the men involved, be they living or dead. I have gone back and looked at pictures of the Taliban men we killed, and reflected on the day, the moment, and the reasons for it all. I find these pictures to be very therapeutic at times, because they force the viewer to remember the emotions of those moments and the sobering outcome of it all.

Most of the guys I know, including me, took pictures of their vanquished opponents. A couple didn't, but not because of general order 1-bravo. Instead, their feeling was more rooted in personal superstitions that such actions would bring about bad luck. Ironically, one of the most vociferous critics in my unit of taking pictures of the dead, or keeping any photographic memory of them, changed his tune after he was almost killed by a suicide bomber. After this bomber blew up near him, he saw fit to collect a small twig of what was left of the bomber's leg bone, and keeps it to this day as a good-luck talisman.

The photos of enemy dead taken by thousands of American soldiers in a dozen conflicts has a historical value both to the individual, as well as the society as a whole. Our history books are filled with stark images of war dead, from the concentration camps of Nazi Germany to the individual American soldiers lying in the sand at Normandy.

Death is an unpleasant but integral part of war, and the photographic evidence of what we did at war should never be censored or banned. I would hope that follow-on generations will have similar photos in their history books so they will not know war as a sanitized experience.

I remember the moment that we had our first confirmed enemy KIA while on a mission. The Afghan soldiers we were with had collected up the fallen man's body, and placed it in the back of one of their pickup trucks. They would deliver it to a local mosque and let the locals deal with the corpse. I was about one hundred meters away from the pickup when I heard word that the body was now in the back of the truck. I knew I had to confront this man who had previously been trying to kill us. I was shaking from a mix of fear of seeing this man close up, and relief that I was still among the living and not laying in that pickup.

I walked the hundred meters to the pickup truck, fighting off nausea and nervous laughter. Facing this man was like facing my own mortality. The closer I got, the more overwhelming it became. By the time I was standing next to him, I was trembling.

He lay there with his eyes wide open, staring up to the heavens. A neatly-cut black beard was tucked under a colorful traditional scarf that he had casually draped over his shoulders and around his neck. He had been hit in the leg and waist, but the wound that killed him was a catastrophic head shot. There was a small hole on one side of his head, and the opposite side of his skull was gone. His head was completely hollowed out. There were no remains of any sort of his brain, just an empty cavern.

It was so surreal, because it looked nothing like any movie I had ever seen. He lay there calmly staring up into the sky. Hours earlier he had risen in the morning like I had, and probably eaten a quick breakfast, then gathered up his gear.

He had likely attended a morning meeting with his comrades, and been briefed on his mission for the day, much like I had. Me and this Taliban man shared a common experience, a common swath of land, and a common job with a common goal. We just happened to be on opposing teams.

I took a picture of him, and I look at it every once in a while when I need to be reminded of how serious this business of war really is.

So I'll conclude this rant against GO-1B, and a confession of our violations of it, with an observation of something that was noticeably missing from GO-1B. Given that the stated goal of GO-1B was to prevent offenses against the host nation's culture, this interesting omission is the permitted importation and consumption of pork.

Pork is banned by the faiths of Islam and Judaism. Pork is seen as an even more offensive affront to the Afghan people's religion and culture than alcohol could ever be, yet pork was still a regular item in all the chow halls across the country. Bacon, sausage, ribs, and pulled pork sandwiches are all on the menu daily.

It won't take you long to find an Afghan who drank alcohol, drinks alcohol, or would like to try it for the first time. But it's nearly impossible to find one who ate pork, or wants to try it. Yet, pork remains perfectly acceptable to the people who wrote up GO-1B. My guess is the final draft of that much-maligned general order was written by some Southern guys who love barbeque, and the thought of going a year without it was something they couldn't stomach, even if it offended the locals.

SENIORITIS

There comes a time when the yearlong combat tour nears its end, and an epidemic of senioritis begins to set in. The symptoms are a euphoric feeling of relief and excitement, coupled with the onset of laziness and a general lack of concern about getting any work done. The computer countdown clock program on Dexter's laptop approaches zero time left. The column of hours, minutes, and seconds expended is full of large, impressive numbers, while the column showing the remaining time left on our year of "boots on the ground" is small, manageable digits. After having watched this virtual hourglass slowly go from one extreme of time to the other, it's an almost orgasmic feeling to see it come to an end, and know that you've survived a year in hell.

You finally begin to see the light at the end of the tunnel, and for once it's not the light from a muzzle flash of a rifle pointed at you, nor the light from an explosion of an IED going off underneath your vehicle.

Since Army regulations forbid the consumption of alcohol in Afghanistan, we can't publicly pop a cork on a champagne bottle to celebrate the end of our tour. Instead, we create alternative ways to mark this pending completion of a year in harm's way. The manner of celebration, as well as the timing of it, varies from soldier to soldier.

Our unit ran the gamut on how to celebrate the end of it all. Some guys threw in the towel about a month before the year was up. And then there were guys like Lancelot, who as already recounted, tried to milk every last drop from his Taliban hunting permit. He was truly the lone member of our unit who dragged out the end to this last possible moment. The vast majority of us had quit days, if not weeks, before Lancelot finally hung up his body armor.

A small group of soldiers formed what I called the Church of the Sun. Led by the charismatic Mr. OCD, his small congregation would meet in morning and afternoon sun tanning sessions. Whenever anyone would walk by his semicircle of tanners, Mr. OCD would offer up his sun-worshipping greeting, which also served as the Church's mantra: "It's all about the base tan," he would say. "It's all about the base tan."

Once the morning suntan session was over, Mr. OCD, like Moses, would lead his followers to the promised land: the FOB's weight room and gym. A short workout would ensue, and then a shower. The whole ritual would be repeated again in the afternoon. What was the point of having a tan if you didn't have the muscle definition to go with it? Mr. OCD made it no secret that he had a lot of dates lined up with future ex-wives when he got home, so it was imperative that when he returned to the States, he hit the ground rested, buff, and tanned.

When it came to tanning, Mr. OCD was meticulous with the timing, sun angles, and rotation of back to chest in the search to get the perfect tan. Tanning, like everything else he did, had that heavy dose of obsessive-compulsive disorder to it.

I'd be a liar to say I never sat out with these sun worshippers to catch some rays. We all got a case of this senioritis to varying degrees. In Vietnam, they called it short-timer's disease. A soldier who only had a couple days to go was referred to as "being short." Here in Afghanistan, we called it a lot of things, but no matter what we called it, openly showing symptoms of "being short" wasn't something that our HQ smiled upon. Guys like Mr. OCD and the Greek and the Falcon had long stopped caring about what HQ thought. They were ready to go home, and their response to complaints that they had thrown in the towel a bit early was pretty straightforward: "What are they going to do to punish us? Send us to Afghanistan?!"

After a year in combat, we were all cocky as hell and tired of the chickenshit. We were itching for a fight with someone above us so we could tell them to go to hell. We were going home soon, real soon, and we just didn't care anymore about playing nicety-nice Army games to satisfy a higher HQ that had failed for the most part to properly support us during our time out in harm's way.

Having said that, there were lots of people who had the same short-timer's symptoms, but didn't go so far as to stick a finger in higher HQ's eye and flaunt it, like followers of the Church of the Sun liked to do. Dexter, Gator, Rainbow, and the Preacher kept up the hard work. They would rail against the sun worshippers, and curse them up and down as being quitters, lazy, or setting a bad example for the new soldiers who were settling in on our FOB as replacements for us.

While I agreed with them, I was somewhere in between the two factions, and I alternated between an occasional tanning session, and a gripe session bitching about the senioritis sun-worshipping slackers.

During the final weeks, the most unpopular guy on the FOB was the one who told us we had a mission. There was nothing worse than the sinking feeling you would get thinking you had to suit up, gear up, lock and load, and go out and risk getting killed in the final days of the tour. I heard many a guy say, "I would have rather gotten killed on the first week than the last, that way I could have avoided all the bullshit in between." There was something about missions during these last days that sent shivers down our spines. Like black cats, broken mirrors, and voodoo curses, they were superstitious harbingers of bad luck and death.

We were all convinced we would get smoked, and we avoided missions like the plague. I think it's fair to say that our last mission, which was a road convoy from our tiny FOB to our corps HQ, was the most white-knuckle ride of the year. There were more nervous smiles and prayers said on that trip than on any that came before it. But fortunately for guys like Mr. OCD and me, the superstitious fears failed to deliver any bad luck to us on this last ride. We made it to our corps HQ, and ultimately back to the States well-rested. And tanned.

Senioritis in effect: Taking a break from work on the final days of our tour. I play a game of chess outside my hootch with my buddy CPT Rolfe.

EPILOGUE

With the rapid increase of troop levels in Afghanistan, the FOBs we lived on back in 2006 and 2007 have quickly been transformed from the small backwater shantytowns we knew, to built-up and modernized places to live. Our dilapidated Russian retread of a FOB that housed only about a dozen American dudes and four hundred Afghan soldiers, is now a major hub of military activity in Ghazni Province. Today there are almost one hundred Americans living and fighting there, and over a thousand Afghan soldiers. The FOB now features a basketball court, complete gym, swimming pool, and modern chow hall.

Security measures have also been substantially improved at this FOB, with the installation of ten-foot high-blast walls and modern fighting positions that make any enemy infiltration extremely unlikely. Gone are the eroded dirt walls, rusty barbed wire, and crumbling Russian fighting positions that kept us up late at night wondering if every creak and squeak we heard was a Taliban soldier about to cut our heads off.

This build up is transforming the habits and lifestyles of the men who live there, and causing twists and turns in the evolution of modern hootch culture. But while a lot is changing, and has changed, I am confident that much has stayed the same. The longing for women, or beer, or other vices of American culture cannot be wished away by Army regulations. The hours of boredom that are the fertilizer for political debates, pranks, and ball-busting continue to fill the days.

The American soldier continues to adapt to and overcome these challenges. The means and methods are sometimes morally questionable and the results sometimes problematic, but the outcome is never in doubt: Dudes will be dudes.

Hootch life has changed a lot over the last few years in Afghanistan, and even more over the last four decades since our fathers fought in Vietnam. The hootchie girl has been re-placed by Internet porn videos. The Dear John letter has been replaced by instant-messaging breakups over a cell phone. The dog-eared paperback novel passed from soldier to sol-dier has been replaced by video games. The cases of cold beer flown in by helicopter to a remote rice paddy are now cases of Gatorade trucked in by private contractors who earn five times the pay of the soldiers who will ultimately drink them.

Back then the typical hootch could have been as sim-ple as a poncho liner and a couple bungee cords. Today, the cords are likely to be Ethernet cables, connecting the modern soldier to the Internet and back to the real world and all its temptations.

I can't predict what the soldier's life at war will be like for the next generation, but I am confident that the spirit and culture of the American soldier will remain as wily, contro-versial and creative as it ever was.

CPSIA information can be obtained
at www.ICGtesting.com
Printed in the USA
BVHW071947300620
582653BV00002B/335

9 780983 051732